UNIONIST SCOTLAND
1800–1997

UNIONIST SCOTLAND
1800–1997

Edited by

CATRIONA M. M. MACDONALD

Foreword by

PROFESSOR T. M. DEVINE D.Litt., F.R.S.E., F.B.A.

JOHN DONALD PUBLISHERS LTD
—————— EDINBURGH ——————

© The Editor and Contributors severally 1998
All rights reserved. No part of this
publication may be reproduced in any
form or by any means without the
prior permission of the publishers,
John Donald Publishers Ltd.,
73 Logie Green Road, Edinburgh EH7 4HF.

ISBN 0 85976 471 0

British Library Cataloguing in Publication Data
A catalogue record for this book is available from the British Library.

Typeset by Pioneer Associates Perthshire
Printed and bound in Great Britain by
Bell & Bain Ltd, Glasgow

CONTENTS

CONTRIBUTORS

Dr Richard J. Finlay
Lecturer in Scottish History, Department of History; Assistant Director,
Research Centre in Scottish History, University of Strathclyde

Dr I. G. C. Hutchinson
Senior Lecturer in History, University of Stirling

Dr Catriona M. M. Macdonald
Lecturer in History, Glasgow Caledonian University

Dr Elaine W. McFarland
Senior Lecturer in History, Glasgow Caledonian University

Dr James Mitchell
Senior Lecturer, Department of Government; Director, Territorial Politics
Research Centre, University of Strathclyde

David Officer
Research Officer, Ulster People's College, Belfast

Dr Graham Walker
Reader in Politics, Queen's University of Belfast

FOREWORD

The past two decades or so have seen a remarkable expansion in both the quality and quantity of important research in Scottish history. Despite the significant progress that has been made, however, major gaps still exist, even in areas which are essential for an overall understanding of Scotland's past.

One such theme is considered in depth in this valuable collection of papers on Scottish Unionism. It can reasonably be said that the Anglo-Scottish Union of 1707 and its consequences over the last three hundred years are the central influence on the shaping of modern Scottish political history. For most of that time the majority of Scots accepted the Union and often voted in large numbers for unionist parties. Large-scale dissent from the Union is a relatively recent phenomenon. Nevertheless, while nationalism and the Labour Party have attracted considerable interest from historians, the study of unionism is much less fashionable. This fact makes this book a truly pioneering collection. For the first time Scottish Unionism has been exposed to systematic enquiry by a team consisting of several established historians and a group of younger scholars. It is particularly gratifying that the idea for this volume developed out of an important conference held at the Research Centre in Scottish History at Strathclyde University organised by David Forsyth and the editor of this collection, Catriona Macdonald. At the time both of them were Ph.D. students in the Research Centre. It is good to see such initiatives from the new generation of Scottish historians for which they deserve warm congratulations.

University of Strathclyde   T. M. DEVINE

1

INTRODUCTION:
THE UNIONIST DISCOURSE

Catriona M. M. Macdonald

> Two hundred and ninety years to the day after the formation of the Union the party of the Union was wiped out in Westminster. Just when the Union faces the biggest upheaval in its history, organised Scottish opposition to its introduction at Westminster had disappeared.
>
> John Curtice, 'New map, new future for Scots',
> *The Scotsman*, 3 May 1997

Defeat has an uncanny propensity to focus the attention of the vanquished on the essence of their being. In the realm of politics, without the patronage and status which come with political success, ideology and tradition reassert their dominant influence at the moment of greatest need as the ultimate features which distinguish – if not unify – a party.

The General Election of May 1997 was such an experience for the Conservative Party. With only 31 per cent of the popular vote, it was the national party's worst performance since 1832 and worst – in terms of seats secured – since 1906. In Scotland this 'nightmare scenario' was of even more dramatic proportions as not one Conservative was returned for a Scottish seat. No matter how much senior Scottish Conservatives attempted to seek consolation in their 'success' in attracting seventeen per cent of the Scottish vote and 'limiting' the swing to Labour to seven per cent – as opposed to the eleven per cent recorded in England – concerns regarding the party's future were quickly translated into a public debate on the ideology of the Scottish Conservative and Unionist Party and its identity as the party of Union.

In the weeks following the election, concerns rested on key dilemmas which reflected long-standing tensions at the heart of

1

Scottish Conservatism and illustrated the apparently contradictory consciousness of a party which, even when in power, had been the choice of only a small minority of Scottish voters. For some, the way forward for the post-'97 Conservative Party in Scotland was a change of name, to reflect its Unionist roots, and the reorganisation of its Scottish operations.[1] For other prominent Conservatives, an explicit commitment to devolution seemed the only way.[2] For many others the answer was to work with Labour's devolution proposals to safe-guard the Union settlement in a new form.[3] Yet there were other factions who maintained that defence of the status quo seemed the only 'principled' way forward.[4] Whilst much was made in the press of such internecine squabbles ('Scots Tories must put their house in order'), the fractures which were appearing in the Conservative ranks were something more than party in-fighting or the petty taunts of cliques.[5] Rather, the debates were generated by serious disjunctures at the heart of Scottish Conservative ideology which were both philosophical and historical in origin.

The Conservatives' post-election interpretation of Labour's land-slide as a victory for devolution in Scotland reflected not merely the 'knee-jerk reaction' of a defeated party, but the opportunity for the articulation of a Conservative Scottish nationalism which, in Blair's Britain, was now at a premium. Scottish Conservative voices sympathetic to devolution, which had been marginalised under Major, ironically seemed to pose as the Conservatives' only hope north of the border.[6]

Was this simply enlightened self-interest? Throughout the Thatcher administrations, the Conservative Party in Scotland had become increasingly identified as an English/anti-Scottish party by the electorate who had been shown to prioritise their dual Scottish/British identity in favour of the Scottish dimension.[7] Consideration of even a lukewarm reception for Labour's Referendum proposals was thus one means of avoiding electoral suicide in a Scotland already devoid of Conservative MPs. Yet a more detailed consideration of how those Conservatives sympathetic to change defended their case in the weeks following the election reveals a party whose conceptualisation of the Union agenda was by no means doctrinally opposed to some degree of self-rule. More than a calculated *volte face*, this position was rooted in the history of (small 'u') Scottish unionism – a contested philosophy, shared by both the Conservative and Labour parties, which had evolved over two centuries in defence of the Union of 1707.

Since 1707, as James Mitchell has made clear, the British state, through the establishment of the Scottish Office (1885) and other distinct legislative measures for Scotland, had become 'a major transmitter of Scottish political distinctiveness'.[8] In this process, Scottish Unionists (between 1912 and 1965 the Conservative interest in Scottish politics had been represented by the Scottish Unionist Party) had been far from unwilling collaborators. Indeed, as the Unionist Secretary of State for Scotland in the 1930s, it was Walter Elliot who masterminded the Scottish Office move from London to Edinburgh and in the 1940s it was again the Unionists who opposed Labour's nationalisation plans as vehicles for greater centralisation and the abdication of industrial control from Scotland to the south of England.[9] Scottish Unionism had thus always sought a distinctive position on the Union.

Things changed somewhat from the 1970s, however, when the inter-relationship of 'successful' SNP electoral challenges and a growing commitment to undifferentiated centralist policies under Thatcher undermined the political premium in 'Scottish' Unionism. Yet, in off-shoots such as the 'Thistle Group' a distinctive Scottish Unionism was maintained. What was 'new' in the post-election fervour in 1997, however, were growing claims in the Scottish Conservative and Unionist Party that Scottish distinctiveness should be allowed to take a democratic form, allowing for the generation as well as the implementation of Scottish policies in an assembly separate from Westminster. Till then the Unionists had accepted difference 'without allowing for democracy'.[10] As Mitchell emphasised in 1990:

> The problem for Unionism has been that, in maintaining a distinctive Scottish aspect, the danger always existed that a demand to incorporate a democratic component would be made or even that the Union should be abandoned. The defence of the Union comes first, before the retention of the Scottish aspect whenever the question is put . . .[11]

Yet how the Union is to be defined is not a simple matter, making its defence a far from straightforward process.

Union as concept

Since 1707, 'the Union' has moved off the page of the Treaty document and become a 'concept', more specifically the point of intersection of a number of important discourses which influenced the Treaty's evolution, its eventual form and consequent interpretation. An imperial discourse, rooted in Scotland's relationship with Britain's position as a major colonial power; a commitment to the stability of the United Kingdom settlement largely focussed on a sentimental attachment to Ulster Protestantism; a surrogate Orange discourse, the power of which waxed and waned with the profile of the 'Irish Problem'; the conflicting local discourses which identified Unionism at a local constituency level; a progressive discourse which drew Liberal Unionism back to its Radical roots; a welfare discourse generated by the growing intervention of the state in the late twentieth century; a civil discourse determined by the growing power of the Scottish Office in the British state and a 'nationalist' discourse in which contrasting concepts of patriotic loyalty wrestled to establish a coherent equilibrium, combined to form a Scottish unionist vision in the 1990s which bore many scars from past battles and encompassed many apparent paradoxes and contradictions. Scottish unionism is and was, both determined by the terms of the Treaty of Union *and* remains more than the sum of its parts. It was generated by discourses which contributed to the Treaty's inception, implementation and historical interpretation. Consequently, at no time was 'the Union' a 'given' in Scottish politics beyond its constitutional and legal parameters, and likewise unionism was always prone to reinterpretation, renegotiation and conflict. As Brown, McCrone and Paterson make clear, identities are not fixed characteristics but are 'negotiated'.[12] This applies as much to the unionist identity as it does to the oft-debated Scottish identity.

Each essay in this volume addresses a significant discourse which has contributed to a unionist vision of Scotland. Whilst treated separately, each author highlights how each theme forms part of a network of issues which have distinguished Scottish unionism as a sophisticated, and at times fragile, complex of inter-related ideologies evolving through time and space. The contributions are ordered to take account of the manner in which unionism possesses both a spatial and historical dimension. From the modern origins of Unionism in the Irish Home Rule Crises of the nineteenth century, we move to the Scottish locality to consider the Unionist Party as a political force in Scotland at a grass-roots level. From here, the volume 'maps' the chronological development of Scottish unionism from the inter-war period to its fractured state in contemporary politics. Each essay highlights the contested nature of Scottish unionism, its powers to unify interests in defence of the Union and its tendency, in so doing, to elaborate a distinctive Scottish dimension in British politics.

'In Ulster the fight is hottest . . .'

T. W. Russell's invocation to his Scottish audience in 1886 to consider Ulster Protestants as 'bone of your bone, flesh of your flesh', high-lighted the manner in which the Ulster question was absorbed as a critical component of late Victorian Scottish Unionism through appeals to tradition, religious unity and a shared history: a process analysed by Graham Walker and David Officer in the first part of their essay in this volume. United further by their common commitment to Empire, Walker and Officer highlight how Ulster and Scottish Unionists (notably Liberal Unionists) participated in promoting an Ulster-Scot agenda in Scottish Unionism throughout the Edwardian period, only to be constrained in their efforts by the cautionary strategies of their Scottish Conservative colleagues after 1912. From this date, the rhetoric of Ulster Unionism began to fade from official Scottish Unionist platforms as the party voiced its support for the Anglo – Irish Treaty of 1921 and attempted to attract the Catholic vote in Scotland in the 1930s. Thus, according to Walker and Officer, the Scottish Unionists avoided becoming a 'tribal mouthpiece' for a militant Protestant agenda. Yet, whilst the authors acknowledge that the Irish question in Scottish politics largely dropped out of sight from the 1920s to the 1960s, they highlight vestiges remaining in the late twentieth century, exemplified by the high Protestant turn-out for the SNP at the 1974 election in protest against Heath's prorogation of Stormont two years earlier and in 1987 when, the authors' claim, the Conservatives were partially damaged by protests over the signing of the 1985 Anglo-Irish Agreement.

The discourses surrounding the changing Scottish Unionist position on Ulster are indicative of a Unionism which had significance outwith Scotland and likewise relied much on external factors to give it shape. The genesis of the Scottish Unionist Association of 1912, emerging as it did from an alliance of Conservatives and post-1886 Liberal discontents, was rooted firmly in a long history of Scottish-Irish relations which predated the Union of 1707. As such Unionist ideology was ingrained with a legacy which at once drew it further into wider debates regarding the territorial integrity of the British state and pulled it further from English Unionist models which relied less on a commitment to Ulster's Protestant minority.

'. . .our principles are not changeable'. . .

The Orange Movement in Scotland was the key vehicle through which a shared Ulster-Scottish heritage was internalised as part of Scottish culture and politics. As Elaine McFarland makes clear in her contribution to this volume, this shared consciousness was instrumental in making Orangemen 'the most trenchant defenders of the Union'. Yet they also posed as 'intractable political allies' for the Scottish Unionists. At root, Orangemen had an instrumental vision of the Union and their commitment to it was determined by the extent to which it defended the increasingly fragile Protestant identity of Scotland. In this way, their support for the Scottish Conservative Party in the nineteenth century, and after 1912 the Unionist Party, was conditional.

The relationship between the Orange Movement and the Scottish Conservative Party was, as McFarland makes clear, seldom an easy one and was continually prone to tension and conflict. Yet the movement's expansion in the mid – late nineteenth century made this relationship an important one for Scottish Conservatives in an era marked by the 'democratisation' of politics. In this period, the Orangemen's 'siege mentality', spawned by their fears of Fenian disturbances, the disestablishment of the Church of Ireland, the 1872 Education Act, the restoration of the Papal hierarchy in Scotland in 1878 and radical Liberal attempts to disestablish the Church of Scotland coalesced with a Conservative predisposition to evangelical Protestantism and the sympathies of many Ulster-born Scottish Tories and their need to attract the working-class vote. Yet fears that 'intimate association with the Orangemen might well block . . . new avenues of support' led to a cooler relationship in the final years of the nineteenth century.

Essentially, the Orange-Unionist discourse was a paradoxical one, according to McFarland. Whilst their commitment to the Protestant religion brought Orangemen into politics, it was also their religion which restricted their political involvement. Echoing the Walker-Officer thesis, McFarland concludes: 'In these difficult circumstances the Orange Order was unlikely to serve as a bond for the Unionist bloc as was the case in Ulster.' The most socially acceptable form of a popular Protestant identity was one shared by all the Scottish political parties and thus had little political capital. To adopt the Orange variant would have isolated more supporters than it attracted and regardless, sat ill with Scottish Unionism's positive enthusiasm for a British state of which Orangemen were becoming increasingly suspicious.

The religious dimension of Scottish Unionism was therefore, like its stance on Ireland, a contested one and failed to fully encompass the complexity of the Unionist sociopolitical vision. Whilst the religious discourse alerts us that there were concerns behind and beyond the constitutional ones which were generated during the Home Rule Crises of 1886 and 1912–14, when analysed, it also illuminates its own limitations.

'. . . *a few faded portraits of the late Mr Gladstone* . . . '

The language of politics provides the focus for my own piece in the volume. Here, the development of local Unionism after 1886 is addressed through the rhetoric of its exponents, the oratory of its opponents and the shared cultural language of the Paisley community. Gladstone's Home Rule declaration of 1886 is identified as an '*un*-defining' moment in the constituency's political past when shared understandings regarding the identities of the major political parties were undermined.

Whilst partly the consequence of the changing industrial and social profile of the town, the dilemmas which emerged in 1886 must be appreciated fundamentally as ideological discourses emerging from the contradictory tendencies at the heart of Paisley's Radical heritage. The Liberal caucus which merged with the Conservatives in Paisley in 1908 took with them the ambiguous legacy of this local history, and injected incompatible interpretations of Paisley's past into the new Unionism by emphasising the movement's contested popular roots. This reinvention of the Radical inheritance as a Unionist antecedent has its parallel in the development of the 'ethical socialism' and progressive Liberalism of the Left in the late nineteenth century. However, unlike the emergent Labour Party, Paisley Unionists were less successful in realising the potential of their Radical roots at the ballot box.

The manner in which such ideological conflicts manifested themselves in language is most evident in the Liberal Unionists' Home Rule, tariff reform and social reform campaigns. Throughout each,

Liberal Unionism, whilst criticised by Paisley Liberals as a cloak for Toryism, defined itself in relation to its reforming roots and the political history of the burgh. As Graham Goodlad has made clear, 'Home Rule was not a policy which automatically commended itself to the average Liberal'.[13] Abandoning the Liberal Party did not mean the Liberal Unionists abandoned Liberalism, nor that their cause would be the *inevitable* victim of Conservative designs on party dominance. The essay traces the evolution of a popular Unionism within Scottish Unionism which, in much the same way as Labourism, owed much to Scotland's Radical Tradition. An unexpected Radical discourse is thus identified at the heart of Scottish Unionism.

'. . . the rigidity of party lines is slackening'

Having presented a convincing analysis of a 'modern' and efficient, though far from universally successful, Unionist Party propaganda machine in the inter-war years, Iain Hutchison illustrates the complex redevelopment of party politics in Scotland in this period. For Scottish Unionists it was a period of negotiation within the party between competing progressive and conservative tendencies now operating within a changing political climate in which the Liberal and Unionist interests had been joined by a third serious contender for office – the Labour Party. In terms of the quality and status of its MPs, it was a 'golden age' for the Scottish Unionist Party, but its victories, according to Hutchison, were less a reflection of its defence of the status quo or anti-socialist agenda than its pragmatic and positive encounter with state intervention and progressive social policy.

Facing two powerful electoral challengers, Scottish Unionists operated tactically at a local level in securing a number of election 'pacts' with the Liberals against their 'Red' opponents. Yet beyond such opportunism, they countered left wing challenges with parallel moderate policies on various aspects of social reform, notably in housing and pensions. Echoing concerns with identity raised in the previous chapter, Hutchison highlights how by the 1930s, many progressive Tories were 'to the naked eye indistinguishable from Liberals.' Moreover, in response to the growing challenge from the SNP, the Unionist Party, according to Hutchison, proved adept at salving Nationalist concerns regarding Scottish representation and treatment within the Union by striving for preferential terms for

Scotland on certain key socioeconomic matters. Reaction clearly had little place in the inter-war party:'Unfettered capitalism was regarded as antiquated in the contemporary economic climate and inimical to social well-being.'

Yet such 'modernisation' left important legacies for the post-war party, as Richard Finlay and James Mitchell highlight in the concluding essays in the volume – essays which should be considered almost as companion pieces.

Tower blocks and 'subsidy junkies'

Moving away from a singular party focus, Richard Finlay devotes his attention to small'u' unionism: 'the belief that Scotland should remain part of the British state apparatus'. Whilst Finlay is critical of Hutchison's interpretation of inter-war Scottish Unionism, maintaining that it was 'defensive and negative' in comparison to its pre-1918 variant, his essay provides a useful bridge to our final concerns regarding contemporary Unionism and highlights the fundamental importance of the economy as a crucial determinant of the style, content and character of Scottish unionism. Specifically, Finlay's thesis rests on an analysis of Scottish unionism in the twentieth century in which he defines its main political justification as its ability to guarantee Scottish economic well-being in a period of world economic and industrial flux. He states controversially: 'economic dependency on England and the British state apparatus have moulded unionist ideology in the twentieth century'.

Identifying three periods of evolution (1918–1939; 1939–79; 1979–1997) during which the Union was alternately treated as a defensive or progressive guarantor of Scottish economic performance, Finlay traces the development of a dependent relationship between Scotland and the 'milk cow' of the Union. From the orthodox economic perspective of the inter-war years which determined a limited governmental role in the economy, through the rise of corporatism and planning in the post-1945 era to the Thatcherite attack on the 'nanny state' after 1979, commitment to the Union settlement was viewed by all the major parties as the sole guarantor of continued Scottish prosperity. Yet, by closely associating corporatism and state intervention with the distinctive hallmarks of Scotland's political culture, this process guaranteed that the Conservative attacks on the welfare state in the 1980s would be identified as attacks on'what was for many Scots, the true essence of a British identity'. By the

1990s, the changing balance of the British and Scottish strands within Scottish unionism had served to undo one another.

'. . . the United kingdom is in danger . . .'

James Mitchell highlights the contested nature of Scottish unionism in the twentieth century by moving from economic determinants of unionist philosophies to the nature of unionism itself as a form of nationalism. By retracing the steps already taken by Finlay, he illuminates theoretical and party political issues not easily encompassed in the'dependency model'which Finlay elaborates, by locating 'change'in theoretical discourses concerning Scottish and British identity and pragmatic party discourses concerning electoral strategies.

Tensions inherent in conflicting interpretations of 'union' and 'unitary' state models of the UK are shown to have influenced the ways in which the Unionist (from 1965, the Conservative and Unionist) and Labour parties have responded to challenges from within their own parties, from the SNP, from the political climate in Ireland and from the socioeconomic health of Scotland in relation to the rest of the UK. Mitchell emphasises:

> Especially over the course of the twentieth century, a substantial gap has opened up within unionism. While agreement remains on the need to cater for Scottish distinctiveness, considerable differences have emerged on how this is best achieved.

According to Mitchell, it is now no longer possible to consider unionism as a cohesive force or indeed the undisputed platform of any one of the Scottish parties.

Unionist Scotland

Brown, McCrone and Paterson, in their influential 1996 study *Politics and Society in Scotland*, emphasised that:

> the UK is not and never has been a unitary and homogeneous political system other than in rhetorical terms. As regards the fortunes of the political parties in Scotland, most obviously since the 1950s, Scotland and England have diverged from each other in support for the two main parties, and second, the parties only succeed in Scotland when they address *Scottish issues*. When they are perceived no longer to do so, they suffer accordingly at the polls.[14]

Whilst history seems to prove the truth of this analysis, it does so only when we accept certain definitions of 'Scottish issues'. Just as Scottish and unionist identities are contested, so the identification of issues relevant or integral to each is by no means straightforward. What distinguishes certain 'issues' as 'Scottish' may just as easily distinguish them as common to a variety of groups across the UK. What makes an issue a 'Scottish' one is dependent on the inter-play of a number of discourses pertaining to political, cultural, constitutional, territorial and socioeconomic factors which are only seldom fully appreciated by political actors and never entirely addressed by any singular party programme. Similarly, it is rare for an issue identified as 'Scottish' to preclude a parallel or complimentary unionist interpretation of the challenge being faced. 'Scottish', 'British' and 'Unionist' are subject positions which too often are accepted as given in debates concerning the legacy of 1707. This volume seeks to address the discourses which together have contributed to the making and remaking of Scottish unionism and treat the legacy of 1707 as that which we need to explain rather than that which frames what is known.

NOTES

1. John Young, *The Herald*, 10 May 1997; *The Herald*, 19 May 1997, *Scotland on Sunday*, 11 May 1997.
2. *The Herald*, 9 May 1997; *The Scotsman*, 9 May 1997; *The Scotsman*, 19 May 1997.
3. *The Scotsman*, 9 May 1997.
4. *The Herald*, 12 May 1997; *The Scotsman*, 10 May 1997.
5. Michael Fry, *The Herald*, 7 May 1997.
6. Note the contrast with the position in February 1992 when, in Glasgow, John Major stressed: 'The danger of Labour's devolution proposals is that they might feed any such grievance, not dispel them. Labour has chosen to ride on a tiger. That tiger, unless soon caged could consume the Union itself.' Speech by Rt. Hon. John Major MP, 'Scotland in the United Kingdom', as quoted by Brendan Evans and Andrew Taylor, *From Salisbury to Major: Continuity and Change in Conservative Politics* (Manchester, 1996), p. 257.
7. Paul Whiteley, Patrick Seyd and Jeremy Richardson, *True Blues: The Politics of Conservative Party Membership* (Oxford, 1994), p. 178; James Mitchell, *Conservative Attitudes and the Union: A Study of Conservative Party Attitudes to Scotland* (Edinburgh, 1990), pp. vii, xiii; David Seawright and John Curtice, 'The Decline of the Scottish Conservative and Unionist Party 1950–92: Religion, Ideology or Economics?', *Contemporary Record*, 19

(1995), p. 334 (See also *Scotland on Sunday*, 29 September 1996; Ian Bell, *The Scotsman*, 27 January 1997).

8. James Mitchell, *The Campaigns for a Scottish Parliament* (Edinburgh, 1996) p. 40.

9. Alice Brown, David McCrone and Lindsay Paterson, *Politics and Society in Scotland* (London, 1996), pp. 15–16.

10. Mitchell, *The Campaigns for a Scottish Parliament*, p. 41.

11. Mitchell, *Conservative Attitudes and the Union*, p. 12.

12. Brown, McCrone and Paterson, *Politics and Society in Scotland*, pp.197, 209.

13. Graham Goodlad, 'Gladstone and His Rivals: Popular Liberal Perceptions of the Party Leadership in the Political Crisis of 1885–6', in E. F. Biagini and A. J. Reid (eds), *Currents of Radicalism* (Cambridge, 1991), pp. 163–164.

14. Brown, McCrone and Paterson, *Politics and Society in Scotland*, p. 120. (My italics.)

2

SCOTTISH UNIONISM AND THE ULSTER QUESTION

Graham Walker and David Officer

'The blood of the Covenanters courses through their veins . . .'

In the development of the Ulster Unionist opposition to Irish Home Rule from the mid-1880s to the outbreak of the Great War, an Ulster Protestant ethnic identity was carefully promoted. It emerged to meet a perceived need for a Unionist challenge to the Nationalist assumptions of the ethnic and racial homogeneity of the Irish. The case against Irish Nationalist designs was imeasurably strengthened when argued in terms of two distinct groups, or peoples, or indeed nations, each with their own claims and aspirations and each with the testimonials of historical struggle to accompany them.[1] Ulster Unionism was in this sense essentially about disruption: it sought to disrupt the coherence and easy fluency of the Irish nationalist view of Ireland as a nation one and indivisible with an historic destiny to be self-governing.

Much of the eventual success enjoyed by the Ulster Unionist movement rested on its ability to cohere and mobilise a heterogeneous population in a series of complex interlocking alliances. This was partly achieved through an appeal to a shared identity and common interest as adherents of the Reformed Faith but the cultivation of an ethnic consciousness replete with its myth of birth, struggle and potential demise played a vital role in suggesting a unity of purpose and experience.[2] A common disposition in the world was advertised which also laid claim to a range of shared characteristics and qualities which had been transmitted through the generations and were as evident in the contemporary protestant population in the North as they had been two hundred years previously.

From the mid-nineteenth century onwards the scrutiny of Ireland's past – geological, archaeological and historical – increasingly became the concern of the gentleman amateur. Employing a new range of scientific procedures to order and codify a variety of relics and artifacts, these endeavours provided much of the raw material through which a grand history of progress from a rude state towards a modern society was narrated. There was a simultaneous concern to capture the living traces of the past believed to be evident in language, dialect and folklore, a project which owed much to the example provided by Sir Walter Scott's literary rendition of Scotland's past derived from contemporary vernacular culture.

Whilst it has been generally recognised that these diverse activities provided a vital source for the development of an Irish nationalist consciousness in general and the Gaelic Revival in particular, much was of potential use to the countervailing force of Unionism.[3]

Central to the ethnic identity fashioned in defiance of Irish nationalist assumptions was the notion of the Ulster-Scots as a distinctive people – a pioneering people with a history of civilising achievement in Ireland, the British Empire and North America. It is in this late nineteenth- and early twentieth-century period – 'The Home Rule era' in British politics – that the myth of the 'Ulster-Scots' or the 'Scotch-Irish' (the term used in America) as a uniquely self-reliant, strong-willed and resolute people not to be meddled with, is significantly cultivated and popularised, both in relation to Ulster and North America. This period witnessed the production of several substantial works on this theme of varying scholarly and propagandist quality. All, however, served the purpose of distinguishing the 'Ulster Scots' from the native Catholic Irish.[4]

The significance of these quasi-scientific codifications does not simply reside in the proliferation of texts devoted to establishing both the historical antecedence of the Ulster Scot and the assumed destiny towards which the group drove. After all, there was a developed sense of difference celebrated in popular songs, parading rituals and other cultural practices which served to distinguish protestant from catholic, planter from Gael and unionist from nationalist. Yet the scientific aura which surrounded these texts, infused as they were with a range of scientific theories (crude Darwinism, racial typologies or physical anthropology), delineated and solidified the boundaries between one group and another in a way which had not been previously achieved.

One such publication, relatively scholarly if partisan, was John

Harrison's *The Scot in Ulster*, published in Edinburgh in 1888. Harrison was a Scot and a historian and he wrote his book after visiting Ulster and being impressed by how 'Scottish', in his view, many of those descended from the settler population remained. His book, it might be said, represents the first coherent textual history of the Ulsterman which, in its romantic portrayal of an heroic people's struggle, supplied the anti-Irish nationalist project with a useful countervailing and mobilising myth and revealed its indebtedness to the tradition of romantic historiography in nineteenth-century Scotland.

For Harrison, the difference between the Ulster-Scots and the Irish had a racial basis. He remarks on feeling at home among his 'kith and kin' with the similarity of names, manners, codes of dress, shop names and whistled tunes. He discerned an essentially Scottish character in areas of Ulster such as County Down with its whitewashed cottages, carefully tended farms and hedgerows. He wrote:

> It shows in the well-ordered little towns, with their broad streets, and well built churches adorned with handsome spires; their busy weekly markets; and that surest sign of a high-class population in their well-washed, clean-pinafored children.[5]

Harrison argued that the Union had at last brought the Ulster Scots their reward: prosperity, good government and security. He saw the Union and the wider Empire as the only context in which better future relations between 'the Scot and the Irish' could develop.[6] Harrison's work celebrated both an Ulster ethnic distinctiveness, with all its potential for Protestant exclusivism, and a concept of the expansiveness of the Union and Empire and their capacity to accommodate ethnic, racial and religious differences. These were indeed two prominent themes in Ulster Unionism in the Home Rule era and beyond and the relationship between them, whilst ambiguous and uneasy, forms an enduring framework for the analysis of the character of the movement.[7]

The 'Ulster-Scot' or 'Scotch-Irish' enterprise was given further momentum by Charles A Hanna's *The Scotch-Irish*, published in 1902. This two-volume work focused largely on the contribution of the Ulster Scots to the development of America and reflected the strong turn-of-the-century interest in the USA in the 'log cabin', 'new frontiers-man' type of image which the 'Scotch-Irish' had acquired. However, this image in many ways crossed back over the

Atlantic, and has been lovingly nurtured by Unionists at particular moments of political crisis as symbolic of their unyielding determination to resist Irish nationalist domination.[8]

Finally, at the height of the controversy over the third Home Rule Bill in 1914, there appeared the Reverend J. B. Woodburn's *The Ulster Scot*. Woodburn was a Presbyterian minister who saw the distinctiveness of the Ulster-Scots as grounded, not in race, but in religion. Significantly, in Woodburn's account Presbyterianism became in effect the religious identity of Ulster Protestantism. The actual denominational divisions and intra-Presbyterian struggles of Ulster's Protestant history were largely elided in the cause of constructing a coherent 'passion play' which would answer the Irish Catholic story with the Ulster-Scot epic: both resonated with the themes of sacrifice, suffering and heroic struggle. Woodburn's tone, in a sense, crowned the whole enterprise conducted by certain Unionists in the Home Rule era: that of controverting the unitary vision of Irish nationalism by counterpoising an alternative national or ethnic origin myth and an alternative interpretation of Irish history. The 'Ulster-Scots' were presented as a people who were the very stuff of the British Empire's civilising mission – the 'cutting-edge' or 'advanced guard' of Empire.

Important examples of Unionist leaders who promoted such notions were the Presbyterian Liberal Unionists T. W. Russell[9] (born in Scotland) and Thomas Sinclair, the latter someone who made much of his Scottish Covenanter origins.[10] It was men like Russell and Sinclair who addressed Scottish audiences at various crisis points in the Home Rule dramas, exhorting them to remember and to respond to their ethnic duties. Russell, in a speech at Grangemouth in 1886, put it as follows:

> Three hundred years ago Ulster was peopled by Scotch settlers for State reasons. You are bound to remember this. The men there are bone of your bone, flesh of your flesh. The blood of the Covenanters courses through their veins; they read the same Bible, they sing the same Psalms, they have the same Church polity. Nor have they proved altogether unworthy of their ancestry. Two hundred years ago when the Empire was in peril, the descendants of these Scottish settlers, hunted from post to pillar, remembering that they belonged to an Imperial race, 'turned desperately to bay' under the walls of Derry and left a by no means dishonourable record of their prowess for the historian. The descendants of these men have made Ulster what it is . . .[11]

Thomas Sinclair is widely held to have been responsible for drawing up the Ulster Covenant of 1912, by which Unionists in their hundreds of thousands pledged to resist Home Rule. The Covenant took inspiration from the Scottish example of the 1640s and this episode is in many ways typical of the way such Presbyterians as Sinclair, many of whom had a Liberal political background, contrived to identify the Unionist struggle with the language and imagery of an essentially Scottish cultural heritage.[12] It was a process which almost rendered those Unionists of English descent invisible, although it might be argued that the Orange Order still conveyed important aspects of an essentially English settler heritage. Nevertheless the Solemn League and Covenant and the appearance of historical works such as Woodburn's constitute something of a 'hi-jack' of the Unionist cause by a tradition by now popularly known as that of the 'Ulster-Scot'.

From Home Rule to Partition

The promotion of the 'Ulster Scot' enterprise was a response to Irish nationalist ideology, but it was also a politically expedient means of attempting to influence opinions in Britain over Home Rule, particularly in Scotland. As has been noted, Ulster Unionists made strenuous efforts to play up the 'kith and kin' theme in Scotland. Their success in this regard, however, was limited.

It appears to be the case that just as in Ulster, it was Liberal Unionists who were largely the most enthusiastic proponents of an Ulster identity which drew so heavily on its Scottish dimensions, so, in Scotland, it was Liberal Unionists who responded most positively to claims of shared interests. One obvious connecting theme here was economics: this was in many ways a show of solidarity between the industrial, commercial and business elites of the west of Scotland and north-east Ulster. The social and economic character of both areas lent itself to intense regional pride and a sense of great self-importance around notions of progress and prosperity. It was also, of course, about economic self interest: both sets of industrialists and traders feared what they took to be the baleful implications of a Dublin Parliament for the industrial and commercial interests of these regions. The Glasgow Chamber of Commerce even considered that a Home Rule Ireland would be a haven for hostile foreign armies and a grave threat to Britain's security.[13] The argument that

Irish Home Rule would strike at the integrity of the Empire was one which signally bound the Clyde and the Lagan Valley. This was the high tide of popular regard in both places for the Empire as the guarantor of social and economic progress and in both places the economic elites tended to be Liberal Unionists, fearful of radicalism but often contemptuous of the conservatism of the rural landed aristocracy.

These Liberal Unionists, fired by Whiggish beliefs in imperial progressiveness, were probably the most enthusiastic adherents of British identity in the UK as a whole. The Ulster Unionist attempts to foster and strengthen the notion of British solidarity found their most positive response in urban west-central Scotland among the Liberal Unionist business circles and the Orange Order-influenced working class. Individuals who typified this 'solidarity with Ulster' line were James Parker Smith, Liberal Unionist MP for the 'Orange' constituency of Partick in the 1890s and 1900s, and John Ure-Primrose, Lord Provost of Glasgow in the 1900s, prominent Liberal Unionist, and a Chairman of Rangers Football Club. The Ulster cause prompted its Scottish supporters to move some way towards incorporating their Scottish national identity in a British variant. In 1895, Thomas Sinclair could feel confident enough of his Glasgow audience's feelings of national identity to draw the following Scottish parallel with the proposed rule of Ulster from Dublin:

> It is just as if it were proposed to transfer the interests of shipbuilders and manufacturers of Glasgow from the Imperial Parliament to the control of a legislature swamped by the crofters of the Highlands.[14]

To some extent, the Liberal Unionists of west-central Scotland might be said to have 'bought in' to the 'Ulster Scot' enterprise which was being promoted in Ulster from the 1880s, sometimes by Scots such as the historian J. Harrison. A Liberal Unionist in all but name by the time he made the following remark in 1912, Lord Rosebery might be taken as representative of this tendency. He said:

> I love Highlanders and I love Lowlanders, but when I come to the branch of our race which has been grafted onto the Ulster stem I take off my hat with veneration and awe. They are, I believe, without exception the toughest, the most dominant, the most irresistible race that exists in the universe at this moment.[15]

The Liberal Unionists in Scotland were prone to portray the Ulster cause in terms every bit as apocalyptic as those used in Ulster itself.

In 1912, at the point of merger between the Liberal Unionists and the Conservatives in Scotland into what would become known as the 'Scottish Unionist Party', the following eulogy and message of support to the Ulster Unionists was minuted in the final meeting of the West of Scotland Liberal Unionist Association:

> In Ulster the fight is hottest. The finest population in Ireland are being driven to extremes, and are imploring our help. They believe that their rights as British citizens, the peace of their homes, the prosperity of their businesses, their religious freedom itself, are all involved in the struggle. No Scotsman could read without deep emotion the narrative of a vast and loyal, population, closely united to us by ties of race and religion, flocking to their churches to implore the most High to avert their threatened danger, and we in the West of Scotland, of all in the British Isles, should hold out a strong hand to them in their hour of distress.[16]

The 'narrative' referred to was likely to have been understood largely as the stirring and heroic saga of the 'Ulster-Scot' seeking moral and indeed practical support from their *heimat*. And, contrary to what is often suggested, there was a significant rallying of Scottish support for the Ulster Unionist cause during the Home Rule crisis of 1912–14, evidenced in large public meetings and demonstrations, Covenant signings, feverishly pro-Ulster newspaper editorials and motions of support passed at specially convened meetings of church presbyteries. Moreover, there are indications that this went beyond traditional Liberal Unionist, Conservative and Orange circles.[17]

Yet the merger between the Liberal Unionists and the Conservatives probably had the effect in time of somewhat damping down the 'solidarity with Ulster' campaign. Certainly, in terms of the expression of such a campaign through the medium of a heightened enthusiasm for British national identity, it can be argued that the Conservative influence was if anything a restraining one. As Richard Finlay has argued, the Conservatives in Scotland were much more circumspect about 'the ditching of Scottish nationality in order to achieve British homogeneity'.[18] They were, of course, impeccably loyalist and pro-British but they were acutely aware of the sensitivities surrounding issues of nationalism and national identity, and of the depth of Scottish national feeling and the potential resentments which might be aroused by attempts to absorb or marginalise it. The Conservatives also appeared better aware of how Scotland's participation in the Empire had intensified Scottish identity and a Scottish

sense of competitiveness *vis-a-vis* England. A Unionist Party memorandum in 1914 stressed the sensitive nature of the Scottish national
question, urged party candidates to try to direct Scottish national
feelings to the ends of Empire, and counselled them to use the
argument that Scottish Home Rule would close off avenues of career
development for ambitious Scots in England.[19] After the merger of
1912 the Unionists, if anything, prioritised issues concerning Scottish
nationality above Ulster, and this became ever more evident as the
Irish constitutional question in general departed the political scene
after 1922.

With their wider geographical base than the Liberal Unionists, the
Conservatives also knew to their cost how deeply entrenched were
the traditional Liberal and often radical political leanings of small
town and rural Scotland, steeped as they were in bitter quarrels over
land and the patronage and disestablishment issues which had
riven the Church of Scotland. Ulster Unionists made a very limited
impact on theise Scottish Presbyterians who felt they could not in
any circumstances align themselves with the Conservatives as the
Liberal Unionists had done. The Conservatives, in short, were more
cognizant of the wider Scottish and indeed British political contexts
and less willing than the Liberal Unionists to subordinate other
political priorities to the cause of Ulster. In contrast to the Liberal
Unionists, the Conservatives were not merely a reflection of the
West of Scotland urban-industrial ethos. Moreover, it was Scottish
Conservatives such as Frederick Scott Oliver who were among those
advocating 'Home Rule All Round' or 'federal' schemes to which
Liberal Unionists were hostile or at best cool.[20] It was largely the
Conservatives, a numerical majority in the new Scottish Unionist
Party after 1912, who ensured that the Party would be guided on
Ulster as on other issues by pragmatic political calculation rather
than emotive 'soul brother' rhetoric. Scottish Unionists, in general,
had always exuded more self-confidence and held more expansive
political visions than Ulster Unionists. The latter, preoccupied with
the quest for security from the threat of Dublin rule, were always
distinguished by a defensive and ultimately narrow and exclusivist
approach to British and Imperial identity.[21]

Scotland, the Northern Ireland State and the 'Troubles'

The extent to which political pragmatism guided the Scottish
Unionists on Irish matters can be measured by the party's support

for the Anglo-Irish Treaty of December 1921. At a meeting of the Central Council of the Scottish Unionist Association in January 1922, a motion endorsing the Treaty was carried and an amendment condemning the government for surrendering to 'the murder gang of Sinn Fein' was emphatically defeated.[22] The issue certainly imposed great strains on the relationship between the Unionist Party and its allies in the Orange Order and other extreme Loyalist circles. Indeed, it resulted in a short-lived breakaway party being formed – the Orange and Protestant Party (OPP). In the 1922 general election, Glasgow Unionists attributed their losses to Labour and partly to the relative lack of supportive Orange Order activity in working class constituencies.[23] However, in spite of the political risks involved, the Unionists faced down Orange disaffection on the issue of the Irish treaty, and indeed on education and on the Catholic Relief Act of 1927.

A close examination of Unionist and popular Protestant politics in the inter-war years in Scotland reveals a clear pattern of protests on the part of extremists generally failing to make headway within the Unionist party, particularly at a senior level. Although there were Unionist 'top brass' who were also senior Orangemen – good examples are Sir John Gilmour (Scottish Secretary of State at various times in the 1920s and 1930s) and Archibald McInnes Shaw (Unionist MP for West Renfrewshire 1924–29) – the party took great pains to prevent itself being perceived as narrowly sectarian and exclusivist in the manner of the governing Unionist Party in Northern Ireland in the fifty years of devolution in the Province.[24] Even in the 1920s and 1930s, when sectarian tensions were high in Lowland Scotland and when much was made by the Protestant Churches and the Orange Order about Irish Catholic immigration into Scotland, the Unionist Party can be found making attempts to win Catholic support.[25] For example, at the 1929 election, certain Unionist candidates gave undertakings of support to the Catholic *Glasgow Observer* newspaper that they would support full state funding for Catholic schools and would support the position of the Catholic Church on birth control.[26] Attempts by Orangemen and Scottish Churchmen to bring about legislation curbing Irish Catholic immigration into Scotland got nowhere either when Labour was in power or when the Unionists, with Gilmour as Scottish Secretary, occupied office.

This is not to say that the Unionists were above playing the 'Orange Card' when they could do so with minimal risk. Nor should it be overlooked that Unionist politics in Scotland until the 1960s drew on an essentially Loyalist 'King, Country and Empire' style of rhetoric and that the Party did not spurn the very significant practical assistance provided by the Orange Order in certain constituencies, the tensions between them notwithstanding. The very active and well-organised women's lodges were of particular value to the Party in this respect.[27] Further, it is not difficult to find evidence of anti-Catholic sectarian sentiments of Ulster vintage in Unionist association records. On the other hand, the bulk of these can safely be read as grassroots outbursts which had the effect merely of allowing the angry rank and file members to 'let off steam'.[28] The Unionists played a substantial role in the 'Orange and Green' aspects of Scottish political culture from the 1920s to the 1960s, but in contrast to Northern Ireland, they avoided becoming a mere tribal mouthpiece and they certainly did not do the bidding of the Orange Order at policy level.[29]

In the Scottish political context from the 1920s to the 1960s, Ulster largely drops out of sight, as opposed to persistent questions of religious sectarian conflict in Scotland which clearly have Irish underpinnings and overtones.[30] The internal politics of the Northern Ireland state did not impinge on Scottish politics as much as religious divisions in west-central Scotland suggested they might have. In keeping with their attempts to keep a check on religious friction, the Unionists in Scotland were not, for example, to be found leaping to the defence of the record of the Northern Ireland Unionist government, even in the isolated moments when the latter's treatment of the Nationalist minority in Northern Ireland was put under the spotlight in Britain. In many ways, this mirrored the relative lack of attention paid by parties opposed to the Unionists in Scotland towards the plight of the minority in Northern Ireland. Nor does there seem to have been much interaction between the Unionist elites of Scotland and Northern Ireland during the period from around 1920 to 1970 – a notable contrast to the situation before the First World War, when the Liberal Unionists in both countries fraternised so closely.

In the post-war period, and in particular during the 1950s when they achieved their highest electoral returns in Scotland, the Unionists may have reaped the benefits of keeping a certain distance from Orangeism and Protestant extremism and eschewing identification with the Ulster Unionists. Recent research by Seawright and Curtice claims that the Unionists got around 29 per cent of the

Catholic vote in Scotland in the 1959 election.[31] Given that the party's performance had been markedly better in 1955 (when they received over fifty per cent of the total Scottish vote) it is likely they received a similar percentage then, if not higher. Such is the capacity of the traditional Catholic-Labour alliance in Scotland to mesmerise observers that this significant amount of Catholic support for the Unionists in the 1950s has been all but ignored by political historians and commentators. However, it must be regarded as a factor in the Unionist successes of this period along with the party's simultaneous ability to appeal to many Protestant working class voters. Other factors bringing about the increase in Catholic support may have included the atmosphere of the Cold War and anti-Communism,[32] but it seems likely that increased living standards and social and economic changes had more to do with it.[33] More work has to be done before firmer conclusions can be drawn.[34]

If keeping a distance from the Ulster Unionists helped the Scottish Unionists build support among Catholics, then it has to be said that such a factor did not prevent what appears to have been a serious decline in that support in the 1960s. Seawright and Curtice suggest that only 17 per cent of Catholics voted Conservative (the Party changed its name in 1965) in the 1970 election. It is just conceivable that the outbreak of the Northern Ireland troubles in 1968–69 was influential in the Catholic community becoming more coherent as a voting block once more but again, it is more likely that social and economic factors were the primary reasons for the change over the course of the decade. Indeed, if the Ulster troubles affected the Conservatives in Scotland adversely it was more likely to have been in 1974 when Orange anger over the Heath government's prorogation of Stormont in 1972 seems to have been one factor in the disproportionately Protestant 'protest vote' which the Scottish National Party (SNP) undoubtedly received in both that year's elections. At an Orange demonstration in Saltcoats in July 1972, the winding-up of Stormont by the Conservative government was labelled 'the greatest and most despicable betrayal in British history'.[35] In addition, in 1987 the Conservatives were, to a limited extent, damaged by protests over the signing of the Anglo-Irish Agreement in 1985 and the formation, by disaffected Orange Order members, of the short-lived and significantly named 'Scottish Unionist Party'.[36]

1990s: Possibilities of Greater Dialogue?

Conservatives and Unionists in Scotland in the 1990s have not generally sought to exploit the Northern Ireland issue in order to arrest their party's electoral decline in Scotland, and win back former constituencies of support in the Protestant community.[37] The spectre of sectarian conflict in Scotland has engendered a deep wariness in all political parties about being identified one way or the other with the Northern Ireland question. Such caution has, if anything, become further entrenched since the Monklands by-election of June 1994.[38] It also seems unlikely that a traditional Unionist approach to the issue would reap electoral dividends in the contemporary Scottish political climate with its restless mood in relation to matters of constitutional reform. James Mitchell's recent survey data suggests that some 45 per cent of Scottish Protestants are, like the vast bulk of Catholics, in favour of a United Ireland as a solution to the problem.[39]

Yet such findings arguably reflect only a pronounced tendency in Scotland, as well as in the rest of Britain, to keep the Northern Ireland issues at a safe distance. They do not reflect any significant degree of careful thought about the problem. In conclusion, it might be suggested that there is something to be gained from fresh thinking on Northern Ireland among all of Scotland's political parties and interested observers. The two places are increasingly linked through consideration of the constitutional options available to them: in both places crucial questions about the viability of the Union; of possible devolutionist and federalist developments; of national and regional identity and of religious and ethnic divisions, demand to be addressed. Engaging with the Northern Ireland debate, on better-informed terms than has been hitherto apparent, could well be a mature and potentially beneficial step for Scots to take independently of the so-called 'Anglo-Irish' structures and frameworks. For Unionists in Scotland in particular there might be an opportunity to help the process of putting the Ulster Unionist case on the broader foundations of cultural pluralism and civic values, and to render less potent narrow concepts of the Union as an ethno-religious cause.

NOTES

Research for this chapter was assisted by a grant from the Nuffield Foundation

1. The frequent slippage between these categories in Irish political discourse was a consistent feature of this period.

2. There is now a considerable international literature which explores these themes. For example, see A. Smith, *The Ethnic Revival in the Modern World* (Cambridge, 1981), and 'Ethnic Myths and Ethnic Revivals', *European Journal of Sociology*, 25 (1984), pp.283–305; B. Kapferer, *Legends of People – Myths of State: Violence, Intolerance and Political Culture in Sri Lanka and Australia* (Washington, 1988).

3. J. Hutchinson, *The Dynamics of Cultural Nationalism: The Gaelic Revival and the Creation of the Irish Nation* (London, 1987).

4. See, for example, J. Harrison, *The Scot in Ulster* (Edinburgh, 1888): W. T. Latimer, *The Ulster Scot: His Faith and Fortune* (Dungannon, 1899): J. Heron, *The Ulster Scot* (London, 1900); C. Hanna, *The Scotch-Irish* (London, 1902); J. B. Woodburn, *The Ulster Scot: His History and Religion* (London, 1914).

5. Harrison, *The Scot in Ulster*, p. 81.

6. *Ibid.*, p. 114.

7. C. Coulter, 'The Character of Unionism', *Irish Political Studies*, 9 (1994), pp.1–24; also R. English and G. Walker (eds), *Unionism in Modern Ireland: New Perspectives on Politics and Culture* (Basingstoke, 1996).

8. See the various publications of the Ulster Society, and the periodical *New Ulster*.

9. Russell's career developed in increasingly radical political directions, particularly around the issue of land reform, and he came to be regarded by Unionists as a dangerous political foe. See A. Jackson, 'Irish Unionism and the Russellite Threat, 1894–1906', *Irish Historical Studies*, 25 (1986–7), pp. 370–404.

10. Sinclair's career is discussed in G. Walker, 'Thomas Sinclair: Presbyterian Liberal Unionist' in English and Walker (eds), *Unionism in Modern Ireland*.

11. Speech quoted in A. W. Samuels, *Home Rule: What is it?* (Dublin and London, 1911).

12. Walker, 'Thomas Sinclair'.

13. J. McCaffrey, 'The Origins of Liberal Unionism in the West of Scotland', *Scottish Historical Review*, 50 (1971), pp. 47–71.

14. *Northern Whig*, 9. March 1895.

15. The quote was used by Woodburn for the frontispiece of his book *The Ulster Scot.*

16. N[ational] L[ibrary] of S[cotland], S[cottish] C[onservative and] U[nionist] A[ssociation] MSS, Acc. 10424/22, Minute Book of West of Scotland Liberal Unionist Association 5 December 1912.

17. G. Walker, *Intimate Strangers: Political and Cultural Interaction Between Scotland and Ulster in Modern Times* (Edinburgh, 1995), Ch. 2.

18. R. J. Finlay, 'Imperial Scotland: Scottish National Identity and the British Empire *c.* 1850–1914', unpublished paper delivered to the annual conference of the Association of Scottish Historical Studies, April 1994.

19. House of Lords Records Office, Bonar Law Papers, 32/3/30.

20. J. Kendle, *Ireland and the Federal Solution* (Kingston and Montreal, 1989).

21. G. Walker, 'Empire, Religion and Nationality in Scotland and Ulster before the First World War', in Ian. S. Wood (ed.), *Scotland and Ulster* (Edinburgh, 1994); also J. Loughlin, *Ulster Unionism and British National Identity Since 1885* (London, 1995), Chs 1 & 2.

22. NLS, SCUA MSS, Acc. 10424/63, Central Council Scottish Unionist Association Minutes, 19 January 1922.

23. *Ibid.*, Acc.10424/73, Minutes, 27 November 1922.

24. For a comparative discussion see Walker, *Intimate Strangers*, Ch. 3.

25. S. J. Brown, 'Outside the Covenant': The Scottish Presbyterian Churches and Irish Immigration, 1922–38', and R. J. Finlay, 'Nationalism, Race, Religion and the Irish Question in Inter-war Scotland', *Innes Review*, 42 (1991), pp. 19–67.

26. NLS, SCUA MSS, Acc. 10424/8, 'File on RC vote 1929–36'.

27. G. Walker, 'The Orange Order in Scotland between the Wars', *International Review of Social History*, 37 (1992), pp. 177–206.

28. See, for example, NLS, SCUA MSS, Acc. 10424/73, Glasgow Unionist Association Minutes 29 August 1927.

29. See Walker, *Intimate Strangers*, Ch. 3 for a comparative analysis of Unionism in Scotland and Northern Ireland in this period.

30. See profile of P. D. Ridge Beadle in file on 'Unionist Whig's Fund' regarding the disappearance of the Irish issue (NLS, SCUA MSS, Acc. 10424/7).

31. D. Seawright and J. Curtice, 'The Decline of the Scottish Conservative and Unionist Party 1950–92: Religion, Ideology or Economics?', *Contemporary Record*, 9 (1995), pp. 319–342. (Some of Seawright and Curtice's findings are based on voters' recall of how they had voted in the past, and thus should be treated with some caution.)

32. See Seawright and Curtice's discussion of the Unionists' use of the term 'socialist', 'The Decline of the Scottish Conservative and Unionist Party'.

33. See R. J. Finlay, 'Unionism and the Dependency Culture' in this volume.

34. See also T. Brennan, *Reshaping a City* (Glasgow, 1959) pp. 126–127 regarding the Catholic vote not being so well organised in the 1950s in the Govan area of Glasgow.

35. Loyal Orange Institution of Scotland, County Grand Lodge of Ayrshire, *Renfrewshire and Argyllshire, Official Programme* (regarding a demonstration to commemorate 282nd anniversary of the Battle of the Boyne), Saltcoats 1 July 1972.

36. T. Gallagher, 'Scotland and the Anglo-Irish Agreement: the Reaction of the Orange Order', *Irish Political Studies*, 3 (1988), pp. 19–31.

37. For a discussion of this issue see S. Kendrick and D. McCrone, 'Politics in a Cold Climate: the Conservative Decline in Scotland', *Political Studies*, 38 (1989), pp. 589–603; and Seawright and Curtice, 'The Decline of the Scottish Conservative and Unionist Party'.

38. Walker, *Intimate Strangers*, pp. 179–184.

39. J. Mitchell, 'Religion and Politics in Scotland', paper presented to the Unit for the Study of Government in Scotland, December 1992. I am grateful to the author for permission to cite these findings.

3

'OUTPOSTS OF THE LOYALISTS OF IRELAND': THE ORANGEMEN'S UNIONIST VISION

Elaine W. McFarland

The electors should not forget that the Orangeman has no politics in the ordinary sense of the word. The religious element is the motive which colours and underlies all his actions. Persecution of the Catholic, i.e. the glorious prospect of hearing their bones 'crunch' in the sack is *the* one aim of the Orangeman's religious and political existence.[1]

This onslaught from the *North British Daily Mail*, characteristic of the bitter political climate of the first Home Rule Crisis of the 1880s, contained an important element of truth from which its target, the Orange Order in Scotland, could not demur. While admitting that its political aims and activities were of considerable consequence, the Order believed that these were the fruit of a deeper religious motivation. The purpose of Orangeism was the defence of the Protestant religion and the Protestant religious settlement in Great Britain and Ireland. Its entry into the political arena was intended to combat the 'disloyalty' of Catholicism – an international church which was believed to be incapable of producing sincere citizens of a nation state.

The essence of Orangeism was contained in this uncompromising position. Thus the Laws and Ordinances of the parent Loyal Orange Institution of Ireland declared that their body was, 'composed of Protestants, united and resolved . . . to support and defend their Rightful Sovereign, the Protestant Religion, the Laws of the Realm, the Legislative Union and the Succession to the Throne of Brunswick, Being PROTESTANT . . .'.[2] In Scotland too, these sentiments found an eager elaboration from the Orangemen's leader, C. I. Paton, who went a step further to proclaim the Order's superiority over degrading political strife:

> It is no mere political participation which is the bond of our Union. The principles which animate us belong to a higher and nobler sphere. Political parties are always fluctuating and changing, their watchwords and battle cries are soon forgotten, but our principles are not changeable and our course of action must be the same, until victory crowns our efforts and till the cry arises, 'Babylon is fallen, fallen . . .'[3]

To analyse the Orange Order's unionist vision and the practical politics which resulted, it is necessary first to grasp this vital religious dimension. The Orangemen's commitment to the legislative Union was only one part of an all-embracing world view which saw history in terms of a Manichaean struggle between heretical Roman Catholicism and 'true' Protestantism. The Orangemen's sensitivity to 'the Protestant Religion in danger' ensured that they would become the most trenchant defenders of the Union, but at the same time rendered them intractable political allies, due to their embattled sense of conspiracy and their abiding fear of 'sell out' by time-serving politicians.

A Rallying Call

It is one of the peculiarities of Irish history that there had originally been a strong Orange lobby *against* the abolition of the Irish Parliament in 1801.[4] When it became apparent that, far from emancipating Catholics, the Union was to function as a buttress of Protestant ascendancy, the Order learned to view its repeal with apocalyptic dread. These fears appeared close to realisation through the manoeuvres of the Home Rule League under the leadership of Parnell. Utilising the newly extended franchise and winning over the Catholic hierarchy in the south, most Irish Roman Catholics were united in the demand for the repeal of the Union. A bill to accommodate this was imminent following the winter election which brought the Liberals to power in 1885.

The prolonged Home Rule struggles which followed from 1885 to 1920 are viewed by many Orangemen as the Order's 'heroic age'.[5] It was now that a revitalised Orange Institution provided an integrative focus for an Ulster Protestant community, divided not only along social and economic lines, but also displaying a remarkable proliferation of ecclesiastical and theological schisms.[6] What Terence Brown has described as 'the myth of the whole Protestant community', a community defined by its determination to resist, was actively constructed during these years, by reference to a common Orange tradition in which Ulster's past was dramatised as a uniformly heroic one.[7] The Williamite campaigns, 'Derry, Aughrim, Inniskillen and the Boyne', as celebrated in the public and private ceremonies of the Order, provided a visual and verbal symbolism, with the dominant motifs of siege and deliverance, which assisted Protestants to express a solidarity of purpose, in short a *'conscience collective'*.[8]

In this role as an ideological fixative the Order was assisted by its interdenominational character, emphasising the shared doctrinal elements of the various Protestant churches, and in a more material vein, by the recurrent economic crises which curtailed the capacity of the working class for independent action. While tensions and contradictions were never entirely absent within the Unionist bloc (as witnessed by the rise of the Independent Orange Order in 1902), Orangeism was available to provide a powerful imagery which legitimated political action against Home Rule and imbued such action with a heartfelt religious fervour.[9] Arguably, the bolstering of ethnic solidarity achieved by the promotion of a heroic past also assisted the development of an Ulster identity with a similar emotional and evangelistic focus.[10] In return, Orangeism itself was able to transcend its earlier limitations to become a respectable religious and political mass movement, retaining a proletarian base, but also attracting membership from the urban professional and commercial classes.

Yet, for all the vigorous rhetoric of the Home Rule decade which cast Ulster as the anchor of Empire, there was recognition amongst the Unionist coalition that the crusade had to be carried beyond the Province. As an organisation which had developed an international dimension in tandem with the Irish diaspora, the Orange leadership was quick to grasp the opportunities for a coordinated anti-Home Rule campaign under the banner of 'Imperial solidarity'. The official position in the Loyal Orange Institution of 1885 was, by the Order's own standards, generous and expansive:

> The Orange Order must secure wider friendly aid and not pose as the sole defenders of imperial unity in Ireland . . . while we bate not one jot of our own conscious opinion, we welcome with cordiality all

who will assist us in keeping intact the bond which united us to the great empire of which we are bound to form a not unimportant part.[11]

In practice, however, it was intended that the chief 'shock troops' in the delivery of this 'friendly aid' were to be their own Orange brethren, working behind existing political forces and mobilising for Protestant defence. In the words of Colonel Waring of Belfast, these men were 'the outposts of the loyalists of Ireland' and the role of the Orangemen in Scotland was to be 'right at the front of the fight'.[12] Not only was the Scottish Order one of the earliest and largest exportations of Orangeism, but it was believed that Scotland was an ancient nation bound to Ulster by bonds of blood, affection and common Protestantism. Moreover, unlike Orangemen in colonial off-shoots such as Canada, Scottish Orange voters might have a useful voice through their representatives in the Imperial Parliament.

Galvanising Orangemen in Scotland in their task were the regular visits from Ulster Orange luminaries such as J. W. A. McCartney, MP for Tyrone, who gave his Glasgow audience in 1885 a pointed history lesson on reciprocal aid:

> A great many years ago Ireland conferred on the West of Scotland the inestimable benefit of instructing them in the Christian religion before the corruptions of the Church of Rome crept into the Christian faith. Scotland returned this gift in the most plenteous and benefi-cent manner by peopling the north of Ireland in the reign of James I . . . There was interchange between Scotland and Ireland, especially between the north of Ireland and this part of Scotland, which had knit the two countries in a bond of brotherhood, commercially, socially, religiously and in relations of consanguinity – in one com-mon bond.[13]

Orange partisans in Scotland were also ready to take up the message of fraternal support. Thus H. A. Long enlivened the 1887 Bridgeton by-election with his typically bizarre motif of 'Derry yet enthroned in her inviolable walls, wondering, gazing across to the sons of the Covenanters.'[14] While, in a more formal manner, the Scottish Grand Lodge officially pledged their movement in 1893:

> to assist by every means in its power, our brethren in Ireland in the campaign they are now waging against the forces of rapine, disorder and disloyalty . . . Should traitors impose on the north the dire neces-sity of civil war, Ulster would muster her sons and the Orangemen of

Scotland would join them and the watchword from rank to rank would be 'No Surrender.'[15]

Yet this ambitious sabre rattling should be treated with caution. The earlier address of the Grand Master, Colonel Saunderson, to the Scottish Orangemen, had more judiciously requested them to put their heart and soul into electoral contests in the interest of Conservative and Unionist candidates.[16] This probably indicates their most realistic course of action in Scotland. Indeed, the contradictions in Orange platform pronouncements beg the broader question of how well the Scottish Lodges were actually equipped to become effective 'outposts' in the Home Rule struggle. Above all, the difficulties which faced the Orangemen in this vital task reflected the limited extent to which the ideology and rich symbolism of Orangeism had survived transplantation to a new national context.

An Uncertain Beginning

Orange political behaviour during the Home Rule crises was more than a pragmatic response to immediate events, but instead drew deeply on historical experience. However, the nature of this experience and the trajectory of the Order's development differed significantly between Ulster and Scotland, a truth which the leaders of the parent body seemed only dimly aware in pursuing their strategy of 'friendly assistance'.

Throughout the nineteenth century, the Orange Order in Scotland was predominantly an immigrant, working class organisation.[17] Orangeism crept into Scotland in a slow and undramatic fashion, intertwined with the process of labour migration from Ulster. The first lodge was established in Ayrshire in 1799, and over the next few decades the movement made uncertain progress in the south and west. Unlike the case in Ireland, the Order notably failed to attract aristocratic representation. Indeed, it would have been surprising if the Scottish gentry had become involved with this exotic import, given their notorious lethargy in support of their own Tory cause.[18] This left the Orangemen in a doubly difficult position. Deprived of upper class patronage, they lacked the protection from legal proceedings often enjoyed by their Ulster brethren, yet at the same time they were unable to separate themselves in the mind of the Scottish public from the landlordist taint of the early Irish Lodges. This was a particularly damaging association, given the poisoned nature of social relationships in many Scottish rural areas.[19]

The Orangemen's only acquaintance with a Scottish grandee was also the occasion of their first foray into Scottish politics: neither was a happy experience. In the early 1830s, the Duke of Gordon was persuaded to act as the figurehead of the Order, in the hope that the Lodges would form the basis of a new Ultra-Tory caucus to stem the tide of reform in Great Britain. These attempts failed in the face of a hostile parliamentary investigation, which also revealed that the Orange rank and file retained a robust interpretation of 'Protestant Principles', militating against simple manipulation for political ends. Even at this early stage of development, proletarian Orangemen greatly preferred a virulent 'anti-Papist' stand against Catholic Emancipation to the more rarefied position of 'Constitutional Defence' and preservation of the rights of property, advocated by Gordon and his coterie. Further Tory interest in the Lodges was not forthcoming.[20]

With development in the political sphere blocked for the present, the Lodges were thrown back on the resources of their grassroots supporters and the 1840s and 1850s saw the upsurge of open faction fighting in the growing industrial areas of Lanarkshire and Ayrshire. While this energetic activity increased Orangeism's public profile in Scotland, it also impressed upon literate opinion that this was a 'violent' as well as an 'alien' importation: in short, 'a Hibernian political fraternity which had outlived the necessity which gave it birth and . . . had too many of the characteristics of a sectarian club to be agreeable to sober-minded Scotsmen'.[21]

Building a Conservative Alliance 1866–1886

The rapid acceleration in fortunes which Scottish Orangeism experienced from the 1860s appeared all the more remarkable for the unpropitious background of previous decades. The second half of the century saw the Order's development and consolidation as ceremonial parades, commemorating the great events of the Orange calendar, replaced violent confrontation as the major form of public activity. Attendances at these events fluctuated, but numerical growth was evident through the 1870s and 1880s, with lodge membership reaching at least 30,000 by the end of the century.[22]

On the surface, this expansion was similar to that of the movement in Ulster but, in reality, the Order had still to transcend its historic weaknesses in Scotland. The Lodges, for example, remained geographically concentrated in the west, with Glasgow and surrounding counties significant growth centres. In contrast, Orangeism in Ulster developed on a broader front in tandem with industrialisation, spreading from its heartland in the border agricultural counties into growing industrial centres such as Belfast. More importantly, the Order in Ulster was also undergoing a qualitative shift in membership, becoming more acceptable to Presbyterians after the disestablishment of the Church of Ireland in 1869. Significant structural change of this kind was much less evident in Scotland, where the Order's mid-century take-off reflected growing Ulster migration rather than expanded recruitment among the indigenous population. Working class Ulster Protestants thus remained the backbone of Scottish Orangeism. The impact of this 'Ulster factor' was also evident in the politicisation of the Order which accompanied its growth from the 1860s.

As Orange membership increased in the West of Scotland, so did the confidence and determination of leaders such as George McLeod and C. I. Paton, that their organisation should become a 'power in the state'. Not only would this secure the continuing progress of the Order itself, it would also advance the cause of Protestantism in the nation's counsels. As Paton expressed it in 1875:

> Thus shall we make our influence felt most powerfully and increase it every day; and gain the cooperation of those who have not joined the brotherhood, but have the cause at heart. How? One, by petitions from each lodge . . .; two, by bringing witness before parliamentary representatives. Those who are already decided in favour of the cause, which a true regard for Protestant interests requires, will thus be encouraged.[23]

Although Paton envisaged an indirect approach in his address, in practice the Order's new assertiveness resolved itself into active support for the Conservative Party in Scotland. This was not unexpected, as Orangemen and Conservatives broadly shared the 'True Blue' imagery of Crown, Constitution and Civil and Religious Liberty, but the alliance which emerged was far from unthinking and inevitable.[24]

The two analyses commonly advanced to explain the support of working class groups, like the Order, for Conservatism are deference and economic self-interest. Both have some validity in the Orange case. The address the Order presented to Lord Salisbury in 1884, for example, was remarkable for its obsequiousness, hailing a 'statesman, who together with the immortal Beaconsfield, secured for England peace with honours . . .'.[25] At the same time, Glasgow Conservatives, seeking support on Orange platforms, made consistent efforts to present themselves as the working man's 'real and true friends'in their capacity as employers of labour. W. C. Maughan typically sought to sway his audience in Blackfriars by reminding them of the large number of measures,'which had raised the social status of working men, which had increased wages, diminished the dangers of life and limb in daily work'.[26]

While these were motivations which might apply to many'working men' of the period, for Orangemen more specific factors linked to their Order's traditional religious mainspring were also at work in shaping political alignment. From the late 1860s there emerged a series of ecclesiastical issues, basically turning on the changing relationship between church and state, which convinced Orangemen that the Protestant platform of William III was seriously imperilled. As George McLeod argued:'it is because the Conservatives as a party occupy this platform and have done so for many years past that the Orangemen claim to be their natural allies'.[27]

These issues were both Irish and Scottish in origin, but in keeping with the ethnic profile of the Lodges, it was the former which exercised the more visceral fascination for the Orange rank and file. Essentially, the Order believed that Papal monarchism and religious absolutism were on the march and that as a result native Roman Catholics had taken the offensive. Two events, causally connected in Orangemen's eyes, signalled this: the Fenian disturbances of 1866–8 – despite their condemnation by the Catholic hierarchy – and the disestablishment of the Church of Ireland.[28] Fenianism even dared to present itself in the heart of Glasgow, and when a demonstration to commemorate the Manchester Martyrs was proposed for Glasgow Green in December 1867, Orange supporters prepared to offer forcible resistance.[29] The following year, Irish Disestablishment became a key electoral issue, and the Order was convinced that Gladstone, under Jesuitical domination, had passed the disestablishment measure as part of an alliance with the Papal party to keep the Liberals in power.[30] Their traditional sense of betrayal activated, the Orange Order organised various protest meetings in the West of Scotland, pledging 'to assist their Irish Protestant brethren in maintaining Protestantism in Ireland against Papal aggression.[31] Accordingly, Orange support was expressed for Conservative candidates in the electoral contest who, in principle, upheld the church and state connection as the cornerstone of national religion, despite their qualms on the actual case of Ireland.

The momentum was maintained during the 1870s and 1880s with further dividends for Conservative links. For many Protestants, the 1872 Education Act threatened the Godly upbringing of the young; for Orangemen, it was further evidence of 'Romanists on the vigil, as ever, attempting to undermine children's moral training by introducing 'the effete Italian superstition'.[32] The appearance of Conservatives such as J. N. Cuthbertson in School Board elections, defending the place of orthodox Protestant doctrine in the classroom was duly noted in the Lodges, while, for their part, the Conservatives realised the value of religious issues in mobilising a growing electorate.[33]

While the Orange sense of siege was reinforced by the restoration of the Papal hierarchy in Scotland in 1878 and radical Liberal attempts to disestablish the Church of Scotland in the early 1880s, the next challenge to put the Orange-Conservative alliance firmly in place was Gladstone's introduction of the 1884 Reform Bill. It might have been expected that a movement with an overwhelming working-class membership would have welcomed a measure which extended the franchise to all male households and redistributed seats to reflect demographic realities. In the event, the Order's preoccupation with the implications for 'the denominational balance of power proved the decisive consideration and the Bill, 'obviously intended to extirpate Protestantism in Ireland', was assailed with desperate rhetoric which prefigured the frustrations of the Home Rule period.[34] As a leading Belfast Orangeman informed his Greenock audience, Ireland 'was in the forefront of the battle', since franchise extension would sweep away Protestant power. In a millenarian vision, he left them in no doubt of the outcome: 'When the smoke of burning households is seen from Galloway and Kintyre – the response would then be prompt and decisive and Ireland would be reconquered by British arms'.[35]

If traditional battle cries shaped the Order's political behaviour in this powerful fashion, what was the Conservative motivation in accepting Orange allegiance? Predisposing factors were the evangelical Protestantism which, as Hutchison notes, coloured West of Scotland Toryism, and the Ulster origins of some leading Conservatives such as W. C Maughan.[36] The most significant attraction of the Order was probably, however, a pragmatic one. The Orangemen's heightened political consciousness came fortuitously during a vital period of transition for Conservatives in the wake of the 1868 and 1884 Reform Acts. The Party could no longer remain the preserve of a landed oligarchy, but was edging towards the status of a modern political organisation with a national electoral framework.[37] Conservatives throughout Great Britain were obliged to face this challenge, but the position of the Party in Scotland appeared notoriously weak to meet the demands of a mass electorate. Perceived as the party of aristocratic reaction, they had failed, as Fry notes, to penetrate the social fabric of urban Scotland: a Scottish National Conservative Association had been set up in 1867, but was a shadow of its English counterpart and did little to build up local support.[38] In these circumstances, the Orangemen provided a quick solution, a convenient short cut to mobilising the lower classes for Conservatism. Not only did successive 12 July parades proclaim the visible expansion of the movement, the Lodges also presented a valuable organisational mechanism, already equipped for the complex business of voter registration and canvassing. It was a further bonus that the attempts of the Grand Lodge from the 1860s onwards to reform the Order's reputation of collective lawlessness, albeit only partly successful, made association with the Orangemen a little more congenial.[39]

The potential of Orangeism to compensate for the deficiencies of formal party organisation is paralleled in the popular Conservatism of the Primrose League. Established in 1883, this body consciously borrowed the hierarchical structure, badges of honour and the mixture of public and private ritual of the Orange Order.[40] Not only did the League function in England as an electoral machine, issuing propaganda and voters' lists but, like the Lodges, its particular strength was in providing a regular round of activities between elections, thus giving an edge over the Liberals whose support tended to fluctuate in line with national political issues. It may, indeed, be a factor in the Primrose League's retarded progress in the West of Scotland that Orangeism was already playing this practical role and resented the newcomer's intrusion.[41] Orange antipathy to the Primrose League was also fuelled by its non-denominational character and the involvement of leading English Roman Catholics like the Duke of Norfolk.[42]

More importantly, there are also two important points of contrast between the organisations which begin to highlight the complexity of the Orange-Conservative relationship. In the first place, the fluidity of politics in the West of Scotland – particularly in the early 1880s – ensured that the efforts of the Orange Order in the Tory interest were a great deal more controversial that the contribution of a few Primrose League habitations. The late 1860s and early 1870s had been perhaps the optimum period for 'organic' links between the Order and the party, as the Conservatives in urban areas such as Glasgow and Paisley commenced the struggle to build a wider popular base. The creation of the Glasgow Working Mens' Conservative Association in 1868, for example, encouraged the active involvement of a gallery of Orange notables.[43] However, as a more effective electoral machinery began to develop, it became clear that the Conservatives' transformation into a mass party could not stop at the co-opting of this constituency. Competition began for middle class as well as working class voters, with overtures in the late 1870s and early 1880s to 'Whiggish' liberals, outraged by radical attempts to reform the House of Lords and disestablish the Church of Scotland. Here, the Conservatives faced a dilemma. Intimate association with the Orangemen might well block these new avenues of support, for as one *Glasgow News* correspondent argued in 1884, Orangeism was still widely believed in Scotland to be:

> the foundation of a religious party, not the fundament of a political one. It would only be fair then, on behalf of all supporters, that less Orangemen prevail on the committees. *It is hurtful to the association numerically, and hurtful to the party politically.*[44]

Nevertheless, the plebeian Lodges had provided tried and tested support and this could not be simply jettisoned in the hope of tactical votes from disgruntled Liberals. A compromise in this respect was only imperfectly achieved. The Orangemen retained an important presence in Conservative ranks and received public acknowledgement in the presentation of Orange addresses to Lord Salisbury on his visits to Glasgow and Paisley in 1884.[45] In other respects, Conservatives were more selective. Significantly, progress in the Conservative-Orange relationship continued in working class wards in Glasgow, but the Orangemen were now only one 'interest' among others in an expanding party organisation and were never to have the ear of Conservative committees and councils the way they had done in the early days of the GWMCA.[46] Indeed, while the Order itself believed that, 'they had shown that the Conservatives could not do without the Orangemen', the mature Conservative Party had become a great deal more circumspect, viewing the Lodges in rather patronising terms, as 'an organised army of industrious, loyal subjects . . . and as such eager and prepared to *cooperate when invited* with Conservative Associations, as allies we can count on, on the day of battle'.[47] The Order's status as a variable in electoral contests received ample confirmation in the 1885 general election, when educational issues offered the prospect of Roman Catholic, as well as dissident Liberal support for the Conservatives. Even Tory candidates who had formerly courted the Order on their platforms now had to tread carefully to avoid irritating the feelings of Catholic electors, 'a great body of men who are followers of Christ with ourselves'.[48]

Nor were the Orangemen, for their part, prepared to become simple political adjuncts. Again, this distinguishes the Order from the Primrose League, whose populist version of pro-imperialist principles was seldom disruptive of the Party's leadership strategies.[49] The fundamental religious dimension of Orangeism stood as a barrier to complete integration with the Party machine and ensured that Orange support for the Conservatives was of a contingent nature, dependent on the latter's handling of 'Protestant issues'. Here, the Scottish Orangemens' position contained definite echoes of the broader 'contractual' relationship between Ulster Protestants and the British state. The 'contract' in both cases entailed elements of mutual obligation and permitted the withdrawal of loyal support from party or state if they were seen to be acting against the interests of Protestant defence.[50]

These tensions were to become more explicit in the following decades but, for the present, the issue concentrating Orange and Conservative efforts was the threat of constitutional change in Ireland.

Opportunities and Constraints: Home Rule 1886–1900

On the eve of the Irish Home Rule crisis, Orangeism in Scotland had already made useful, if uneven, political progress in the shape of a working relationship between the Orangemen and the Conservatives hammered out from the 1860s. Certainly, the Order, as an 'imported' organisation, had experienced greater success in this respect than with other pillars of Scottish civil society, such as the churches. The threat of Home Rule was also to bring an immediate boost for the Lodges: at the 12 July demonstration of 1886, for example, a much increased complement of over 10,000 marched from Glasgow to Cowlairs.[51] Moreover, in contrast with general Scottish opinion which had been little stirred by the issue before 1886, the Orangemen were well attuned to a measure which they read as simply the latest and most threatening of Popery's assaults on Protestant rights.

The Order was now, however, faced with a political scene in Scotland which was experiencing rapid change in party alignments. Gladstone's Home Rule Bill destroyed the Liberal Party's precarious unity and gave rise to the new Liberal Unionist grouping. These developments resulted in a more distinct polarisation of political ideology and a more explicit class basis for party politics than else-where in the United Kingdom. The professional and business classes, whose support the Conservatives had long coveted, formed the basis of the new Unionist party and the Tory press quickly urged an electoral pact.[52]

The alliance which resulted was eventually to produce a genuine breakthrough for the Scottish Unionists. By 1900, the Liberals – for the first time since 1832 – were no longer the majority party in Scotland.[53] In the short term, the Unionists' electoral impact was not as dramatic as elsewhere in the United Kingdom, nor was the Conservative-Liberal Unionist pact as harmonious. Given disputes over candidate selection and much organisational friction, it seemed in the 1880's that only the negative dynamism of opposition to Irish Home Rule kept the parties in harness and fears that some Liberal Unionists could easily defect back to the Gladstone camp were never far from the surface.[54]

In these difficult circumstances, the Orange Order was unlikely to serve as a bond for the Unionist bloc, as was the case in Ulster. Three major problems intervened in Scotland which, taken together, illus-trate the cultural and ideological limits to the transplantation of the Orange tradition.

The most obvious difficulty was that the Order's 'Boyne Water' symbolism did not have the same emotional potency in its country of adoption. As an Irish Orangemen writing in the *Scottish News* in 1887 understood it:

> The events of the Revolution of 1688 did not make such a marked impression on the memories of the people . . . as of Ireland. For while the feelings of Great Britain soon quietened down, they were kept alive in the Sister Isle by a continuation of that danger which at the Revolution was only forced into abeyance.[55]

It was the very timeless quality of the myth of siege and heroic defi-ance that had given it its power in drawing together the various strands of Ulster Unionism, but this same appeal to unchanging certainties and constant threats was less appropriate for Scottish latitudes, even if laced with a liberal 'dose' of 'common Covenanting forefathers' from Orange platforms. For example, while it was true that the events of 1688 to 1690 had secured the Scottish Kirk in its Presbyterian form, the church-state relationship had been the focus of much bitter controversy and reform attempts since those times, not least in the decade preceding the Home Rule crisis. Single-minded Orange rhetoric avoided such complexities.

Equally perplexing and inhibiting to the Orangemen was the fact that while 'common Protestantism' certainly coloured the Unionist bloc in Scotland, it was not unique to it.[56] The supporters of Irish Home Rule, who remained true to Gladstonian principles, were also overwhelmingly Protestant. Scottish Liberalism had indeed long been sustained by radical Presbyterian values. These too found expression in more radical bodies such as the Scottish Land Restoration League, whose commitment to land reform lead to an active alliance with Irish nationalists and the Land League.[57] Even the leader of the Irish Home Rulers in Scotland, John Ferguson, the chairman of the Glasgow Home Government Association, was an Antrim Protestant who, like many Orangemen, had left Ulster as an economic migrant in the 1860s.[58] Faced with this 'treachery' from their co-religionists, the best that could be done in the initial stage of the Home Rule struggle was to remind them that 'it behoved all true Protestants to set themselves with all their might to the resistance of Popish aggression'.[59] The issue was eventually to resurface in the 1911 to 1913 Home Rule crisis when, as Walker notes, it lead to a determined attempt by Ulster Unionists to influence 'progressive' Scottish Presbyterian opinion through a Convention held in Belfast in February 1912.[60]

These vexations were compounded by a third problem in the process of cultural transmission. Essentially, the Orangemen were spearheading an attempt to transplant the defensive mentality of Ulster Protestantism into a Scottish context, where imperial unity and Protestant mission were interpreted in more positive and outward-looking terms. Although Scottish self-confidence and self-image was not to peak until perhaps the 1912–14 constitutional crisis, this was true even in the 1886 Home Rule struggle, when an economic depression allowed some propagandists to threaten an influx from destitute Ireland if the imperial connection was broken.[61] Essentially, the Orange articulation of the benefits of imperial unity had a character distinct even from that of their political allies, the former embattled and negative, the latter more expansive and positive.

The Orangemens' opposition to Irish Home Rule was total and implacable, drawing on their distinctive vision of reality. This was founded on uncompromising 'anti-Popish principles', and fired by their perception of the previous twenty years as a period of increased Papal encroachment. Their sense of threat was given a desperate edge, since the site of the struggle between Catholicism and Protestantism had again shifted to Ireland. For the Orangemen, the real root of Ireland's political crisis was in the religious affiliation of the mass of her people and the hold over them exercised by the priesthood. It was the priests, 'the curse of Ireland', who stood behind political agitators like Parnell and Davitt, their strategy being that, 'any old stick will do to beat a dog with, using the Land League to knock the Protestant church.'[62]

Grand Master Paton had already developed this analysis in an excited state: 'What are the evils that affect Ireland? – Popery! If the Bible were better known and read there, there would by fewer outrages'.[63] He went on to condemn the Liberal administrations of the past for their pandering to disloyal subjects:

> Each concession made in the hope that . . . it would satisfy the papists and make Ireland peaceful. And what was the result? Peacefulness, loyalty, content? No! But louder and still louder cry the daughters of the horseleech, Give, Give! The truth must be spoken, the British government and legislature had not been faithful to the Protestant Constitution of Britain . . .

Within the Unionist bloc in Scotland, this determined, 'theological' opposition to Home Rule was complemented by more subtle and complex views on the constitutional nature of the Empire. As Fry notes, the most violent Scottish opposition was not directed at *Irish* Home Rule as such, but at Gladstone's subordinate proposal that Irish MPs should be excluded from Westminster.[64] If this precedent was followed for Scotland, it could mean exclusion from the imperial arrangements, to which – as Richard Finlay highlights elsewhere in this volume – she had brought such industry and energy and which were considered the touchstones of economic advance. Sir John Pender, shipbuilder and Unionist candidate for Govan, expressed the position in 1889: 'The relation between Clyde-side industries and the maintenance of the Union is . . . strikingly intimate. The maintenance of Empire is vital for on it depends commerce. The unity of the country is desirable for the entire community and particularly for working classes'.[65]

The most creative thinking on the issue of the imperial connection came from the Liberal Unionists, whose commitment to a general measure of devolution for the United Kingdom, including Scottish Home Rule, helped demarcate them from their Conservative allies. For Parker Smith, the candidate for Paisley in 1886, the alternatives for Ireland were not Home Rule or coercion, rather, the choice was between 'a good and a bad scheme of self-government, between one leading to strife and separation, and one drawing closer together the bonds of union of the three kingdoms'.[66] Of particular offence to the Orangemen was the coupling of this 'constructive' position with further material concessions to Ireland, as advocated by another prominent Liberal Unionist, Cameron Corbett, who proclaimed that 'our great hope for the future peace and prosperity of Ireland must rest on the peasantry becoming owners of their own holdings on the one hand, and their enjoinment of full education on the other.'[67]

More to the Order's taste was the forthright condemnation of constitutional change which issued from Conservative ranks, especially from party activists who shared living links with Ulster. James Hamilton, 'as an Irishman', informed the Glasgow Conservative Association in 1886 that, 'to give any measure of Home Rule was a complete surrender by the Liberal government . . . the industrious and prosperous people of Ireland were far more opposed to Home Rule than the people of England and Scotland – most people were thoroughly loyal to the backbone'. He concluded in stirring verse:

> Shall rebellion be triumphant,
> And shall the Union die.
> Then two hundred thousand Ulstermen,
> Will know the reason why.[68]

This instinctive and dogmatic position was not, however, the sum of Conservative opposition to Home Rule, which also had important economic and constitutional motivations. The behaviour of Irish Nationalists and Land Leaguers, and Gladstone' collusion with them were seen not only to threaten the rights of property in Ireland, but also to undermine these rights in the whole of the United Kingdom. Many Tories would have agreed with Somervell of Sorn when he succinctly explained, 'it is not a question of religions, it is a question of measures'.[69] Thus, Home Rule was also viewed as running contrary to the growing sense of British national pride and the urge for imperial consolidation which had been fostered by the Conservative party from the 1870s. Here, Ireland was viewed as the integral part of a great nation. For Somervell, it was 'the brightest jewel in the Imperial Crown', and not simply the first line of defence in the preservation of the Protestant religion, as the Orangemen believed.

These differing emphases were unlikely to lead to open conflict during the Home Rule struggles, but they are indicative of a degree of uncertainty in Orange-Unionist relations which was not always evident from official pronouncements. The official Orange attitude to the Liberal Unionist-Conservative pact was one of decided approval, the threat to the Union outweighing other irritations, such as some Liberal Unionists' adherence to the cause of Scottish disestablishment. In a more positive sense, the constructive social and labour policy contributed by the ex-Liberals to the alliance was also welcomed by the Lodges' working class membership.[70] Accordingly, the next ten years saw an abundance of resolutions, pledging the Order's 'unabashed confidence' in the Unionists and its 'determination in supporting them in refusing the Irish Nationalists a separate parliament'.[71]

In practice, the Liberal Unionist component of the electoral pact were more circumspect over their new Orange links. This was unfortunate for the Order's political ambitions, since it was the ex-Liberals who were initially to provide much of the Unionists' organisational muscle, as well as their distinctive ethos of progressive imperialism.[72] This shift was already signalled in the 1886 election, when the Orangemen found that many of their key areas of political strength, such as Blackfriars and Tradeston, now had the new party's candidates at the helm. While the Orange influence was absent from Liberal Unionist electoral committees and councils, the party were content to use the Orangemen in an instrumental fashion in contests where they were calculated to provide the maximum benefit and the minimum embarrassment. In Govan in 1881 and again in 1895, for example, Orangemen were actively 'shipped in' from outside the constituency (from Belfast in the latter case) in the apparent hope of boosting the Liberal Unionist's profile as the 'working man's' candidate. 'What can the Scottish working men of Govan think?', queried the hostile *Mail*.[73]

More commonly, a discreet public distance was maintained. The ignorant and unruly reputation which was firmly attached to the Order from its inception in Scotland was most unwelcome to the middle class membership of the Liberal Unionists. Unlike their Conservative allies, whose Orange links were well established, their recent experience as Liberals in successive elections had done little to mitigate the impression that , 'the Orange elector will sell his birthright (suffrage) secured by Liberal governments, like Esau, not exactly perhaps for a mess of pottage, but often for a glass of whisky or an ounce of tobacco'.[74]

There were also strategic objections. In the mid-1880s, as Hutchison suggests, the permanency of the Liberal schism was not apparent to actual participants.[75] In the volatile political situation of the times, it was viewed as imperative for the Liberal Unionists, not to merge with the Conservatives, but to retain their distinctive identity as anti-Home Rule *Liberals*. Only this course would tempt Gladstonian Liberals and encourage wavering supporters to vote tactically for a Tory candidate, as required in some divisions. This independent stance would hardly be encouraged by high profile involvement from the Orangemen, who were regarded as the most extreme and objectionable auxiliaries of True Blue Toryism. For Liberal Unionist candidates besieged by well-meant offers of 'Irish loyalist lectures', these calculations meant some polite manoeuvring.[76]

In contrast, for the moment the Order's relationship with the Conservatives remained congenial, although not all lodge members had mastered the complexities of the new political arrangements: in Govan one excited Orangeman rose, in the midst of a Liberal Unionist meeting, and sang: 'We are the boys, the Tory boys'.[77] These sentiments received recognition from the party in the decade following the first Home Rule crisis. The Orangemen maintained their localised strength on Conservative committees in divisions such as Bridgeton, where Orange links were well established, while Conservative politicians were less inhibited in publicly acknowledging Orange support.[78] A precedent had been established in Ayrshire in 1890, when Conservative agents for the county had appeared in person at the Kilmarnock 12 July demonstration, rather than sending polite apologies as in former years.[79] By July 1892 J. S. Maxwell had become the first Conservative candidate in Glasgow to address a District Lodge meeting, and this same general election also created the first 'Orange' MP William Whitelaw.[80] Whitelaw had won the constituency of Perth on a split vote, proclaiming that 'he had the honour to belong to the body of Scotch Orangemen, and there was no better organisation on the Unionist side'.[81]

This developing public rapport was probably assisted by the fact that a new generation of Conservatives, like Whitelaw, were coming to prominence by the early 1890s, who identified less with the pejorative reputation of the Scottish Lodges', but glanced admiringly at the vital role the Orange Order was playing as a populist Unionist bulwark in Ulster. In addition, Whiggish Liberal assistance, which had caused qualms over Orange adherence in the past, had no longer to be actively courted, but was already in place through the Liberal Unionist electoral pact. Such were the local irritations and tensions implicit in this arrangement, especially in the West of Scotland, that the Conservatives were not about to jettison their Orange allies.

As in the 1870s and 1880s, this was progress within definite limits for the Order. The greater visibility of the Orangemen in Conservative campaigning was set against a further phase of expansion and growth in confidence for the party. The West of Scotland Tories were no longer an apologetic and marginal grouping, among whom an active and vocal Orange presence was bound to loom large. Change was not only at work within the party, however. Increasingly in the 1890's the Orange Order in Scotland began to assert itself as an autonomous pressure group within the Unionist camp, with its own distinct agenda of 'Protestant issues'. This was signalled by the publication of separate Orange election manifestos in 1892 and 1895, albeit requesting the brethren to support Unionist candidates.[82] Here, the impetus came from within the Grand Lodge leadership. As with the Conservatives, this reflected the emergence of a 'new guard' who were more likely to countenance an independent attitude to their political allies since, unlike men like George McLeod or Thomas Wetherall, they had not personally nursed Conservatism in its early stages of growth in the West of Scotland.

This capacity for autonomous action was to be realised from 1895 onwards, just as it seemed Orange-Unionist relations were set to flourish. In fact, the return of a Unionist government with a resounding majority and the receding prospect of constitutional change for Ireland, provided the perfect opportunity for the Orangemen to scrutinise the performance of their political allies more closely.

Again, the catalyst was a set of politico-ecclesiastical issues which seemed to place the Protestant faith in danger. In the first place, the

Unionists in office had continued to pursue a policy of conciliation in Ireland, 'killing Home Rule by kindness'. This had been Lord Salisbury's policy in his first two administrations, but was now given more eager application by Joseph Chamberlain and the Liberal Unionists who advanced an extensive programme of public works. Characteristic of Unionist strategy was the 1896 Land Act and, particularly contrary to Orange sentiments, A. J. Balfour's plan to establish a 'Catholic' university in Ireland. Secondly, the Unionists were also anxious to reconsider the financial position of voluntary schools. While this was most relevant to English Non-conformists, in Scotland it was seen to be of most benefit to Catholics who would, in effect, receive rate support for educational provision. The third point of contention was the vexed issue of 'ritualistic' or quasi-Roman Catholic practices in the Church of England. To extirpate these, the Church Discipline Bill was introduced in 1897, banning Mass and Confession in the Anglican Church. This received strong support from the Liberal leader, Sir William Harcourt, but the Unionist government was not energetic in its efforts to see the Bill passed, and put to a free vote it was unsuccessful.

The Orange Order was outraged by these transgressions. The Unionists' initiatives, or lack of them, appeared as a betrayal of the electoral support the Orangemen had consistently given them. The 'contract' which had brought the Order into party politics was broken, as the Unionists appeared to have run down the standard of True Blue Protestantism and adopted a 'pro-Romanist' policy. The Order's wrath was swiftly voiced by the Grand Lodge leadership. The Grand Master, William Young, presiding at the 12 July celebration in 1897 declared:

> Orangemen would only support a Conservative candidate where they supported Orange principles. In the last election Orangemen were the means in the West of Scotland of returning a great number of Unionist candidates and expected great things of a Unionist government. In the name of the Orangemen of Scotland, he begged to inform the Unionist government that they would not receive their support if they attempted to pass a bill for the benefit of Roman Catholics in Ireland.[83]

Protestants were even more fearful the following year, as Orange conspiracy theory swung fully into operation. Reverend Townsend reminded his Bellshill audience at the 12 July celebrations in 1898 that the enemies of Protestantism were not only the Land League and the Papal hierarchy, but were to be found at work *inside* parliament. Indeed, their Unionist allies had turned out to be mere politicians, 'who could come to their Orange soirees and talk a lot of amiable nonsense, but when Protestantism was at stake they sat like a lot of dumb dogs . . . Let them as Protestants be neither Conservatives or Liberals in the future, but Protestants first and foremost'.[84]

For a moment it seemed that George McLeod's prediction that the Order was was 'willing to go with any political party, who would uphold the principles which they upheld', would be fulfilled.[85] In this case, however, the Order's alienation was only temporary, as more pressing dangers intervened. The general election of 1900, fought against the background of the South African War, raised the prospect of a further Irish Home Rule Bill, if the Liberals were returned. Liberal opposition to ritualism was eclipsed by their 'pro-Boer' reputation in Scotland, where the Party's radical, pacifist strain reasserted itself. In these extreme conditions, the Grand Lodge neatly shifted its position to align behind the party of patriotism. As William Young on this occasion explained:

> As they knew the Orangemen had always supported the Conser-
> vatives and were thankful that they had supported that Party when
> they took account of South Africa. He counselled his audience
> therefore to support that Party, which he was convinced had the best
> interests of the country at heart.[86]

This episode was the beginning rather than the end of the Orange Order's suspicion of political Unionism. Even the future champion of Ulster Protestant rights, Andrew Bonar Law, was not exempt from charges of acting 'contrary to Protestant principles and practices'.[87] In the new century, the pattern of estrangement and rapprochement was to be repeated as dissatisfaction with government performance and new 'Popery Bills' drove the Orangemen to consider independent Protestant political organisation, 'unfettered' by party ties.[88] The fact that these political adventures failed, and the Orangemen were usu-ally driven back into the Unionist fold, reflected a central fact of the Order's experience in Scotland; namely that, despite its developing profile during the later nineteenth century, the movement had failed to undertake that same journey from the periphery to the centre of social and political life experienced by its Ulster counterpart. It was perhaps the Orangemens' own realisation of this weakness that prevented more ambitious and damaging forays in the independent pursuit of 'Protestant issues' in Scottish politics.

NOTES

1. *North British Daily Mail*, 2 Aug. 1887.
2. *Laws and Ordinances of the Loyal Orange Institution of Ireland*, (Dublin, 1896), p. 1.
3. *Glasgow News*, 23 Jan. 1875.
4. R. Foster, *A History of Modern Ireland* (Harmondsworth, 1987), pp. 284–5.
5. See, for example, R. M. Sibbett, *Orangeism in Ireland and throughout the Empire* (Belfast, 1939).
6. P. Brooke, *Ulster Presbyterianism, The Historical Perspective 1610–1970* (New York, 1987).
7. T. Brown, *The Whole Protestant Community: the Making of Historical Myth* (Belfast, 1985).
8. See G. Walker & D. Officer, 'Scottish Unionism and the Ulster Question' in this volume.
9. D. Roberts, 'The Orange Order in Ireland', *British Journal of Sociology*, 22, (1971), pp. 269–82.
10. For a brief summary of the growing debate on the development of Ulster nationalism, see G. Walker, 'Empire, Religion and Nationality', in I. S. Wood (ed.) *Scotland and Ulster* (Edinburgh, 1994), pp. 101–3.
11. *Glasgow News*, 22 Dec. 1885.
12. *Irish Protestant*, 25 Nov. 1902.
13. *Glasgow News*, 6 Nov. 1885.
14. The *Mail* described his contribution as 'Orange balderdash'.
15. *Glasgow Herald*, 10 July 1893.
16. *Glasgow Herald*, 29 June 1892.
17. E. W. McFarland, *Protestants First: Orangeism in Nineteenth Century Scotland* (Edinburgh, 1990), pp. 47–95.
18. M. Fry, *Patronage and Principle: A Political History of Modern Scotland* (Aberdeen, 1987), p. 90.
19. I. G. C. Hutchison, *A Political History of Scotland 1832–1924* (Edinburgh, 1986), pp. 10–1.
20. McFarland, *Protestants First*, pp. 55–61.
21. University of Glasgow Special Collections, Robertson MSS, J. McConechy, 'Draft of a Memoir of William Motherwell', (n.d.).
22. McFarland, *Protestants First*, pp. 70–85.
23. *Glasgow News*, 23 Jan. 1875.
24. This was particularly true of the Conservative party of the 1870's who preferred this traditional stand to the development of novel policies. M. Pugh, *The Making of Modern British Politics*, Second Edition, (London, 1993), pp. 53–7.
25. *Glasgow Herald*, 1 Jan. 1884.
26. *Glasgow News*, 16 Oct. 1885.

27. *Glasgow News*, 10 March 1880.
28. E. W. McFarland, 'A Reality as Yet Implacable: Perceptions of Fenianism in Mid-Victorian Scotland', *Scottish Historical Review*, (1998). (Forthcoming).
29. *North British Daily Mail*, 12 Dec. 1867.
30. *Glasgow News*, 8 Oct. 1874.
31. *Glasgow News*, 29 Oct. 1868.
32. *Glasgow News*, 29 Jan. 1874.
33. Hutchison, *A Political History*, pp. 120–2. The Grand Lodge made an explicit commitment of support in the 1874 general election for Conservative candidates Whitelaw and Hunter who had put the school issue at the head of their electoral addresses, *Glasgow News*, 19 Jan. 1874.
34. *Glasgow Herald*, 22 March 1884.
35. *Glasgow Herald*, 8 Nov. 1884.
36. Hutchison, *A Political History*, p. 120.
37. Pugh, *The Making of Modern British Politics*, pp. 44–53.
38. Fry, *Patronage and Principle*, p. 90; Hutchison, *A Political History*, pp. 113.
39. McFarland, *Protestants First*, pp. 147–57.
40. M. Pugh, *The Tories and the People* (Oxford, 1985), p. 13. It rejected the 'lodge' appellation, however, in sensitivity to potential Roman Catholic recruits.
41. *Ibid.*, pp. 128–33. *Glasgow Herald*, 14 Nov. 1884 noted that the League had not caught on in Scotland, the only 'habitation' being in Paisley, though a warrant had been recently obtained for the 'Montrose' no. 216 Habitation in Glasgow.
42. *Ibid.*, p. 45.
43. See, for example, Glasgow Working Men's Conservative Association Annual Report 25 Jan. 1870, Conservative Offices, Edinburgh. *Glasgow News*, 2 Dec. 1868, 5 April 1868.
44. *Glasgow News*, 25 July 1884. (Original emphasis.)
45. *Glasgow News*, 1 Oct. 1884.
46. Some working class Conservatives were also anxious to distance themselves from the Orange taint and protested in 1877 that, 'there are working men, as well as Orangemen, who are Conservatives', *Greenock Telegraph*, 21 Dec. 1877.
47. *Glasgow News*, 4 Nov. 1884. (My italics.)
48. *Glasgow News*, 23 Nov. 1885. A further indication of the limits of Conservative rapprochement was the reluctance of most party members to actually join the Order. The establishment of the lodge Beaconsfield's Purple Guards in 1880 to capture a 'better class of recruit' and promote Orange-Tory links was not a success: McFarland, *Protestants First*, p. 145.
49. Pugh, *The Tories and the People*, pp. 11–20.
50. For the development of this contractual concept see M. Elliot, *Watchmen in Sion: The Protestant Idea of Liberty* (Belfast, 1985); and for its application in Ulster, D.W. Miller, *Queen's Rebels* (Dublin 1978).
51. *Govan Press*, 17 July 1886.
52. *Scottish News*, 12 May 1886.

53.	Hutchison, *A Political History*, p. 193.
54.	*Ibid.*, pp. 208–10.
55.	*Scottish News*, 16 July 1887.
56.	There were, of course, also exceptions in Ulster to the identification of Protestantism with opposition to Home Rule, such as Rev J. B. Armour: see R. B. McMinn, *Against the Tide: J. B. Armour, Presbyterian Minister and Home Ruler* (Belfast, 1985).
57.	T. W. Moody, 'Michael Davitt and the British Labour Movement 1846–82', *Royal Historical Society Transactions*, 5 (1953), pp. 53–76; J. Hunter, 'The Gaelic Connection: the Highlands, Ireland and Nationalism, 1873–1922', *Scottish Historical Review*, 54 (1975), pp. 178–204.
58.	For Ferguson's obituary see *Glasgow Observer*, 6 Jan. 1906.
59.	*Glasgow News*, 13 July 1886.
60.	Walker, 'Empire, Religion and Nationality', pp. 105–15.
61.	*Ibid.* For later anti-Irish sentiments see also, *National Union Pamphlet No. 3*, 'Promise versus Performance', (1892). This type of propaganda placed the Irish brethren in the Order in Scotland in a sensitive position which their opponents tried to exploit. The Unionist candidate for Paisley, C. N. Johnston was asked at a public meeting whether he was not prepared to grant self-government to Ireland, 'to allow the Orangemen to go back to that land which gave them birth'. He replied he was quite willing to leave that question to the Orangemen who had left Ireland: *Glasgow Herald*, 21 June 1892.
62.	*Glasgow News*, 12 March 1886.
63.	*Glasgow Herald*, 13 July 1884.
64.	Fry, *Patronage and Principle*, p. 108.
65.	*Glasgow Herald*, 7 January 1889.
66.	*Scottish News*, 21 June 1886.
67.	*Glasgow News*, 25 June 1892.
68.	*Scottish News*, 25 Feb. 1886.
69.	*Glasgow News*, 6 Nov. 1884.
70.	*Glasgow Herald*, 12 July 1886.
71.	*Glasgow Herald*, 15 July 1888.
72.	See C. M. M. Macdonald, 'Locality, Tradition and Language in the Evolution of Scottish Unionism' in this volume.
73.	*North British Daily Mail*, 5 January 1889; 17 July 1895.
74.	*North British Daily Mail*, 2 August 1887.
75.	Hutchison, *A Political History*, pp. 154–85.
76.	McFarland, *Protestants First*, p. 196.
77.	*North British Daily Mail*, 5 January 1889.
78.	Glasgow Conservative Association Annual Report 1899. There were 5 Orange Vice-Presidents in Bridgeton, for example.
79.	*Glasgow Herald*, 14 July 1890.
80.	*Glasgow Herald*, 5 July 1892.
81.	*Glasgow Herald*, 6 July 1892.
82.	*Greenock Telegraph*, 29 June 1892.
83.	*Glasgow Herald*, 12 July 1897.

84. *Glasgow Herald*, 12 July 1898.
85. *Glasgow News*, 13 July 1881.
86. *Glasgow Herald*, 9 July 1900.
87. *Daily Record*, 2 October 1900.
88. McFarland, *Protestants First*, pp. 213–4.

4

LOCALITY, TRADITION AND LANGUAGE IN THE EVOLUTION OF SCOTTISH UNIONISM: A CASE STUDY, PAISLEY 1886–1910

Catriona M. M. Macdonald

The discovery that Harold meant to stand on the Liberal side – nay, that he boldly declared himself a Radical – was rather startling; but to his uncle's good humour, beatified by the sipping of port wine, nothing could seem highly objectionable, provided it did not disturb that operation. In the course of half an hour he had brought himself to see that anything really worthy to be called British Toryism had been entirely extinct since the Duke of Wellington and Sir Robert Peel had passed the Catholic Emancipation Bill; that Whiggery, with its rights of man stopping short of ten pound house-holders, and its policy of pacifying a wild beast with a bite, was a ridiculous monstrosity; that therefore, since *an honest man could not call himself a Tory*, which it was in fact, as impossible to be now as to fight for the Old Pretender, and could still less become that execrable monstrosity a Whig, there remained but one course open to him . . . in these hopeless times, nothing was left to men of sense and good family but to retard the national ruin by declaring themselves Radicals, and take the inevitable process of changing everything out of the hands of beggarly demagogues and purse-proud tradesmen.[1]

George Eliot, *Felix Holt, The Radical*

The operation of history and ideology are indivisible and it is in the discourses which emerge from this relationship, rather than in any static conceptualisation of 'party' or 'programme', that political identities are continually shaped and reshaped.[2] Throughout, the language of discourse is both generative and reflective of 'new' concerns which seek their place in a pre-established political 'geography', and integral to the tensions which emerge in the appropriation of the past by competing party interests through their alternative elaborations of 'tradition'.[3] The meaning of such discourse, however, is bound by a spatial domain within which such a 'cultural language' has resonance with a shared past. Thus the power of 'community', as a defining factor in political partisanship, emerges as a key determinant of political identity.[4]

The ways in which locality, tradition and language shaped political discourse in the town of Paisley in the twenty years following Gladstone's declaration in support of Irish Home Rule highlight the processes through which the elaboration of popular and meaningful interpretations of the past became critical in the articulation of a meaningful political vision of the future. '1886' shattered a pre-existent – if increasingly fragile – consensus on the *meaning* of Liberalism, Radicalism and the Radical Heritage of the town and facilitated the creation of competing languages of reform, one of which was popular Unionism.

Locality

In their studies of the 1980s, Clarke, Dickson and Speirs identified an established political and class consensus at the heart of Paisley Radicalism in the early nineteenth century: a consensus based on shared value systems and the traditions of small-scale independent textile manufacture. A feature of this consensus was the blurring of class distinctions due, in the early years, to the relative ease with which a weaver could establish himself in business, and in a later period, to the fears of the weaving community of sublimation into the growing army of factory 'hands'.[5] Clarke and Dickson have identified this concentration on 'common interests' as critical in determining the predominantly reformist nature of Radicalism in Paisley in the first half of the nineteenth century. In particular, employers and weavers

> worked together to oppose those interests which they saw as being mainly responsible for Paisley's troubles. These were the inadequate representation of the people in Parliament and the domination of the landed interest, particularly in relation to the Corn Laws. Over such issues as the Reform Bill it was almost a 'natural' alliance of working class leaders and local employers who spearheaded the enormous popular enthusiasm in Paisley for change.[6]

Yet such a powerful reformist bloc co-existed with more 'covert' forms of proletarian action, committed to revolutionary and republican ideologies.[7] Clarke and Dickson thus identify a pattern of political expression which 'oscillated'

> between demands for reform of the system (which brought together sections of the working class with the 'advanced' Whigs of the local employers and professions) and more directly oppositional forms of action (which tended to frighten away local manufacturers).[8]

Here, the 'common interests' of reformism sit awkwardly with the 'competing interests' of revolutionary sentiments, evident in the scale of support in Paisley for the General Strike call during the Radical War of 1820. Quite simply, the political culture of the artisan elite contained 'contradictory tendencies'.[9]

In the long term, it was these conflicting susceptibilities which, by promoting incompatible interpretations of Paisley's Radical Tradition, led to the subsequent assimilation of many of its elements in the alternative doctrines of Gladstonian democracy, post-1886 popular Unionism and, of course, Edwardian Labourism. The mechanisms influencing such change were complex. The changing nature of capital accumulation and the considerable capital investment needed to compete successfully in the local textile trades which, by the late nineteenth century, were becoming dominated by large scale thread production, were of prime importance, as was the shift in male employment away from textiles and into the metal and engineering industries.[10] As a corollary, the subsequent female domination of the thread industry resulted in the segmentation of the local labour market into primary (skilled, male) and secondary (unskilled, female) sectors across which the old values of the 'weaver interest' proved ineffectual in achieving any unifying 'class' or cultural influence. The 'common interests' and 'common culture' integral to the consensual politics identified by Clarke and Dickson were thus undermined within and across the classes which had traditionally composed the Radical interest.

By substituting a reform agenda 'domesticated' by party Liberalism,[11] the industrial paternalism of the thread employers, J. & P. Coats and Clark & Co., together with the ethos of respectability which dominated the practices and philosophy of the skilled unions in the mid-late nineteenth century, succeeded in containing the tensions which industrial transformation encouraged within popular

Radicalism.[12] Yet such industrial changes only contributed to tensions originating elsewhere in the realm of ideology.

Tradition

As Doreen Massey's research has made clear, spatially uneven effects in industrial geographies are partly produced as a result of 'historically prior social uses of space'.[13] Whilst this formulation is useful in appreciating patterns of change over time in particular industrial communities, a simple appeal to such an evolutionary model ignores the popular application of conflicting *meanings* to each stage of development by positing an uncontested continuum. It is only by exploring popular perceptions of historical developments (whether industrial, political, social or cultural) that local identities and their political expression may be appreciated.

Isolated spatially and appreciated as the partial consequence of economic and industrial imperatives, local political identities must be located in the processes which evolve and transform local tradition. Tradition – a concept rooted in the associational life of the community – has the power to legitimise *change* in a number of ways: by identifying it with an idealised or actual past; by absorbing change materially, through its incorporation in secular rituals and local institutions; and by accommodating it linguistically within the community's 'cultural language'. As Calhoun has made clear, 'Actual social practice and tradition are interrelated and mutually determining.'[14]

The political changes which originated in 1886 – particularly the creation of a separate Liberal body in the Liberal Unionist Party – sought accommodation within Paisley's Radical Tradition and were likewise shaped in the popular mind by that tradition itself. National politics were appreciated through the distorting lens of local concerns and local traditions and were expressed in a local language which itself was a historical creation.[15] Popular Unionism both benefited and was restricted by its dependence on such local traditions, but as such was as much a beneficiary of the Radical legacy in Scotland as the emergent Labour Party – the party commonly identified as the inheritor of this dissenting past.[16]

Recent work by Patrick Joyce has highlighted the manner in which the 'plebeian invention of tradition' fused Liberal sentiments and socialist thought, thus drawing radical Liberals into the Independent

Labour Party. Yet Joyce fails to appreciate how in certain instances popular Unionism traced a parallel course, fusing local Radical traditions with an appreciation of the potential of Empire and Union as vehicles guaranteeing national and universal liberty, civilisation and good government.[17]

Language

> New kinds of relationship, but also new ways of seeing existing rela-
> tionships, appear in language in a variety of ways: in the invention of
> new terms; ... in the adaptation and alteration (indeed at times
> reversal) of older terms ... in extension ... or transfer. But ... such
> changes are not always either simple or final. Earlier and later senses
> co-exist, or become actual alternatives in which problems of con-
> temporary belief and affiliation are contested.[18]

Raymond Williams' appreciation of the non-linear relationship between historical and linguistic change, whilst stopping short of attributing a *creative* (as opposed to reflective) capacity to language, succeeds in pointing to an appreciation of change in history which exists both within and beyond the word.

'Radical', 'Liberal' and 'Unionist' are subjects which so far have been presented in this narrative as essentialised positions. Likewise 'Radicalism', 'Liberalism' and 'Unionism' have stood as given, incon-testable and contrasting – either / or – ideologies. Whilst not denying the *effects* and operation of such identities, it is only through an appreciation of such identities as historical linguistic creations that we can appreciate the nature of the processes through which such categories emerged and changed over time. By making the language of politics that which we need to explain rather than that which elements our explanation, the manner in which local traditions accommodated and resisted change is made manifest and conven-tional resorts to 'class' explanations are called into question.

The simple acceptance of 'Liberal' and 'Unionist' as political labels distinguishing distinct and sharply differentiated political visions in the late Victorian period underestimates the complexity of the process of realignment which was operating in these years. Recourse to a static vision of Liberal philosophy which identifies Liberal Unionism as an aberration is also unhelpful. As Graham Goodlad has made clear from the English perspective:

Irish Home Rule was not a policy which automatically commended itself to the average Liberal. The Parnellite's record of obstruction in the 1880–1885 Parliament and their opportunism in directing Irish voters to reject the Liberals in the 1885 General Election; the long-standing anti-Catholic strain in English Nonconformity; the association of Nationalism with violence and illegality in Ireland: these factors scarcely predisposed rank and file Liberals in favour of such a policy departure.[19]

Similarly, the identification of 'working class' Unionism as political deviancy is likewise flawed. Popular Unionism reflected less a mode of political deviancy or a contradictory consciousness among workers than the expression of broader sociopolitical concerns which were rooted in the same insecurities that motivated early Labour activists. As Alan Lee has made clear:

> such men and women . . . were no eccentric fringe . . . their ideology was not just an interesting paradox. They were rather an integral part of the development of working class ideology during a period when the stresses of a maturing economy and the strains of an emergent democracy were having their greatest effect.[20]

In what follows, three critical themes which shaped the dominant concerns of late nineteenth-century Unionism in Paisley will be considered: the Home Rule crisis, tariff reform and social reform. Whilst each theme encompasses its own distinct concerns, each exposes complementary threads in the linguistic transformation of Paisley's Radical Tradition and the generation of a related popular Unionist vision of the past.

Home Rule

On 26th April 1886 the Paisley Liberal Club debated the Government of Ireland and Irish Land Purchase Bills, presented to the Commons by Gladstone earlier that month. On a division it was agreed by 75 votes to 40 to support the motion of the local soap manufacturer, and future Liberal MP, J. M. McCallum: 'That Paisley Liberal Club thanks Mr Gladstone for his noble attempt to settle the Irish grievances and trusts that the Government proposals will form a satisfactory basis for legislation.'[21]

In terms of unqualified support for Gladstone, the resolution is somewhat ambiguous and is illustrative of the way in which the

Liberal Party on the ground had for many years sought to contain conflicting power groupings within the party: both those manufactured at a national level (Whig, Liberal, Radical, Imperialist, 'Little Englander', Unionist) and those which evolved from local, municipal concerns. In this instance, however, the attempt at reconciliation was futile. Although the Paisley Liberal Unionists chose initially to fight their cause from within the Liberal Club in an uneasy alliance with the local Conservatives and Beaconsfield Club, a separate Paisley Liberal and Radical Unionist Association (PLRUA) was established in April 1887.[22]

The general election of 1886 highlighted major points of disjuncture which would eventually lead to the split in the local Liberal Party and, in many ways, represents the first stage in the process of the public definition of Liberal Unionism in Paisley. Throughout, the new political 'union' attracted the scorn and satire of its opponents. *The Paisley Chronicle* described the platform party at one of the Liberal Unionist campaign meetings as

> truly a motley and ill-assorted group; old fashioned Tories; Tory Democrats from the Beaconsfield Club; and Liberal Churchmen, the pillars of the church Defence Associations . . . the Paisley adherents of Mr Goschen . . . and the members of the Which school who worship Lord Hartington . . . two or three renegade Radicals.[23]

The split from the parent body was thus neither as immediate nor as straightforward as current historiography would suggest, likewise, any definition of its identity is problematic.[24] Even at the inauguration of the PLRUA, Ex-Provost Clark maintained: 'They were now as they formerly were – Liberals'.[25]

The 1886 campaign, however, focussed on the ill-defined figure of the 'Liberal Unionist' and the emergence of a new party grouping in Paisley as the most direct manifestation of the crisis which had entered Paisley politics. James Parker Smith, the Liberal Unionist candidate in the 1886 election and the Liberal candidate for West Renfrewshire as recently as 1885, mounted a campaign platform in Paisley in June 1886 to be greeted with the shout 'A Tory with a *new name*'.[26] Similarly, to William Barbour, the sitting Liberal MP, Parker Smith fitted none of the established 'types' upon which party politics were structured: 'he could be all Liberal or all Tory. The *name* he preferred himself was Unionist, and he might be said to represent the Tories and Liberals in an equal degree'.[27] The Liberal Press were likewise apprehensive of this new political 'hybrid', noting: 'any *so-called* Liberal, who is the nominee of the Beaconsfield Club and the choice of Mr Goschen's Paisley Committee has *no right to the name of Liberal.'*[28]

By contrast, Parker Smith and Unionists throughout the 1880s and 1890s, posed a parallel 'logic', focussing on older Radical commitments to constitutionalism and class-cooperation: themes which dominated the earlier reformist traditions of Paisley Radicalism. At a Unionist demonstration in the Clark Town Hall in Paisley in November 1887, J. P. B. Robertson MP addressed the crowd:

> We have to face not merely the rage of the faction which thrives upon poverty and adversity in Ireland, but we have also to face the apologists and defenders of the general cause of lawlessness – the Gladstonians of this country.

The aim of Unionism, he claimed, was 'the protection of civil rights'. 'Law', he said, 'is not merely the great shield of the poor as distinguished from the rich, but it is the expression of the voice of the community in determining what shall be done within its bounds'.[29]

Thus, in constitutionalism the Unionists found an alternative critique of the Radical concept of 'Justice', encouraging Ex-Provost Clark to announce in 1890: 'now the Conservatives and the flower of the Liberal Party . . . were bravely marching in line, conquering cruel tyranny, giving protection to the weak, and inspiring confidence in the minds and hearts of the weak'.[30]

Class co-operation, wedded to a rhetoric which focussed on civic and imperial unity further enhanced this alternative Radical vision of Unionism. At a meeting of Paisley's Parliamentary Debating Society in 1894, the prospective Unionist candidate for the burgh, Alexander Moffatt, stressed that

> the Unionists were entitled to call themselves more than the Unionist party; they were entitled to call themselves the National Party. Their Party embraced all the elements of the Nation . . . while their opponents' party embraced only a section of the nation, and that not by any means the best section.[31]

Beyond this vision of Union, the Empire also had radical potential. One week later, Moffatt took up the theme:

> It was strange that men should exist whose minds were so warped by their petty prejudices that they could not see that the British Empire was the most potent instrument for good in the world; that its extension meant the extension of good government and good

order, of peace, of law, *and of liberty*; that its power meant prosperity for the people of this country and for millions of poor, more or less savage people throughout the world . . .[32]

The appeal to 'good government', the criticisms of 'petty prejudice', the demand for liberty and a commitment to a form of internationalism all resonate with earlier Radical rhetoric, most notably that which was to be found in the 'Chartist' Sermons of Paisley's Patrick Brewster.[33]

The oratorical emphasis on the language which could justifiably be used to define the new Unionist ideology, the questioning of labels and the conflicting interpretations of 'Liberal', 'Union' and 'Empire', illustrate the importance of language as a critical element of the realignments which 1886 necessitated. Words clearly did not merely represent a crisis going on elsewhere, they themselves at once embodied and created that crisis, importing confusion into the party structure as existing words and definitions seemed ill-suited to emergent new interests. Definitions were thus recreated, interpretations modified to accommodate aroused sensibilities and local precedents sought for the attribution of new labels.[34]

As Lawrence has acknowledged:

> democratic parties are invariably broad-based coalitions, within which one can identify a wide range of ideological traditions. At particular historical conjunctures one of these traditions may capture the levers of power within the party, but even then its political success is likely to rely in part on the survival (and mobilising ability) of other ideological traditions.[35]

Clearly, 1886 saw a nationalist 'tradition' triumph in the Liberal Party and a pre-eminent commitment to a Unionist vision guide others into an apparent political 'no-man's land'. Yet in order to defend their respective positions, *both* bodies had recourse to appeals to a former Radical age when ideologies seemed 'fixed' and identities established. In the years which followed, the shared commitment to this common heritage perpetuated tensions at the heart of Paisley politics – tensions elemented by questions of language and identity.

Tariff Reform

Tariff reform was the ultimate expression of Paisley's Radical Unionism in the Edwardian period, not simply as an exemplar of 'principled opportunism'[36] or an attempt to 'cut the ground from under the Labour Party', but as a redevelopment of a Radical heritage from which certain conservative Liberal Unionists had been tempted to stray since 1886.[37] Paisley is notable in Scotland in these years for the number of industrialists who were explicitly committed to tariff reform. Archibald Coats and W.H. Coats were both at the founding meeting of the Glasgow and West of Scotland branch of the Tariff Reform League and the latter would later be found on its Executive Committee.[38] Yet tariff reform achieved its greatest significance in Paisley by throwing into relief the tensions which had always existed within the Unionist 'camp'.

In November 1902, John Moffat of Ardrossan, a recent candidate in the Elgin Burghs constituency against Asher, the late Solicitor General, was adopted as the Unionist candidate for Paisley. Described as 'a young politician of promise' by the West of Scotland Liberal Unionist Association (WSLUA), Moffat's commitment to tariff reform attracted controversy from the beginning. In 1903, whilst the Business Committee of the WSLUA maintained an 'open mind' on the fiscal question and explicitly lent support to Balfour's Sheffield programme, Moffat unsuccessfully exerted pressure for a more resolute position, and at a meeting that December called for 'a further resolution of approval of Mr Chamberlain's policy'.[39] However, meeting with further failure the following year in his attempts to attract support for 'some resolution of a decidedly whole-hogger tendency', Moffat came to focus his attention on constituency matters.[40]

In 1905, Moffat delivered an address to a crowded meeting in the Clark Town Hall where he represented his commitment to tariff reform as a defence of workers' rights:

> In all directions it was the aim of the capitalist to take advantage of the undefended condition of the labourer, to force him to work the longest hours for the least pay, to keep a check on him as regarded education . . . to turn him as much as possible into a tool or machine, and finally, to take from him the right of combination and the power to resist the extortionate demands of his employer. he said it with sorrow and regret . . . he said it to urge them to see that no efforts are spared to induce Parliament to pass remedial measures . . . before the rights of the working classes have been forever lost and swallowed up in the encroaching tide of militarism, capitalism and the other 'isms' which are threatening them.[41]

From the floor, a voice declared, 'You talk like a Radical'.

The language was that of the independent artisan, and the focus was the familiar condemnation of the exploitation of rank, privilege and position. The appeal to rights ('the undoubted rights and privileges of the working classes – privileges which they, in common with all free men, had possessed from time immemorial'), the emphasis on 'fair play', and the evident fear of a return to an age of political 'slavery' are distinct echoes of a Radical past. In Paisley, Moffat articulated tariff reform principles in a language more akin to trade unionism than Conservative Imperialism. He appealed to the working man at work-gate meetings, urging him to abandon Free Trade just as he had abandoned individualism in the workplace. Tariff reform, he suggested, was nothing more than the elevation of this principle to the realm of international politics.[42] Replace the capitalist manager who failed to give a fair day's pay for a fair day's work with the foreigner who employed 'slave' labour and set up tariff walls against British goods, and you had a working definition of tariff reform which drew on the sectional impulses which were part and parcel of trade unionism's contribution to the Radical inheritance. Seen in this way, Protectionism was little more than 'the protection of labour and the defence of traditional values and a traditional way of life'.[43]

The extent to which Moffat's brand of popular Unionism was successful in Paisley may be gauged from the membership of the local Liberal Unionist organisations in the town. Whilst the Conservatives had taken the lead in organising clubs to attract a broader base of support in the locality, Moffat together with his agent, Ernest Druce, were foremost in developing a corresponding Liberal Unionist network of support. Throughout Moffat's time as Unionist candidate in Paisley, meetings and demonstrations were held on a more regular basis, ward committee membership increased and a Committee of Management was established within the PLRUA to co-ordinate propaganda. In 1904, Druce boasted of a membership of one thousand and whilst we must be cautious of accepting this partisan estimate, there is no doubt that he was right when he emphasised that even in 1904, the PLRUA was becoming 'a highly efficient political organisation.'[44]

Moffat's influence on local Unionism was, however, far from universally popular. Rumours of a split in the Unionist ranks over Moffat's style of candidacy emerged as early as December 1903 and were further encouraged when he was appointed President of the PLRUA in March 1904 (with Druce as Secretary). Matters came to a head when, in December 1904, Moffat addressed a demonstration in Paisley and attacked his opponents within the local party as 'nominal Unionists', denounced the Conservative Campaign Guide and declared 'the only real living power in British politics' to be Mr Chamberlain.[45] By February 1905, sixteen vice-presidents of the Liberal Unionist Association had resigned office, along with Lord Kelvin, the Honorary President of the Association; the Duke of Abercorn (Honorary President of the Beaconsfield Club) had withdrawn his support; Chamberlain had distanced himself from Moffat's controversial attacks on the Balfour ministry and both the Eastern Unionist and Conservative Associations had declared themselves opposed to Moffat's continued candidacy.

Yet Moffat was, for a time, undaunted. In February, he wrote to the *Daily Record*, stating that Balfour was unfit to hold office due to his inability to 'understand or appreciate the needs and the thoughts of the working classes'.[46] In May, he addressed a Paisley meeting, describing 'Mr Balfour's Cabinet of Nonentities' as representative of 'all that is truly and in the worst sense reactionary in political tradition'.[47] Yet, by June Moffat's position had become untenable, and on the 15th he resigned. In a communication to the press, he noted that it had 'dawned on (his) mind that a Unionist candidate is one who is expected to defend and maintain existing abuses, and all that makes for social inequality' and concluded that tariff reform was a policy to 'enslave the masses'.[48]

The press reflected on Moffat's candidature and his subsequent 'conversion' to Liberalism as a joke and a 'fiasco' ('Moffat Madness'). However, Moffat's concerted assault on Whiggish tendencies in Paisley Unionism and his 'reidentification of Unionist interests with those of the working classes', are intrinsic to any understanding of how the legacy of 1886 lasted beyond the end of the nineteenth century.[49] Moffat's reassertion of the Radical roots of Liberal Unionism is indicative of a process of political realignment which had been necessitated by the Home Rule legislation of 1886 yet which was still incomplete in the Edwardian period. Clearly, 'fluidity rather than rigid dogmatism characterised popular interpretations of party differences in these years, and highlighted the continued inadequacy of the political labels which had evolved through the attempted institutionalisation of older genuinely plebeian traditions.' [50]

Moffat's populist Unionism illustrates how Paisley's Radical heritage worked against more conventional Liberal/Labour interpretations when its defensive and collaborationist elements were brought to the fore. Ultimately, after 1886 'the Radical Tradition was no longer the exclusive property of the Liberals, but a depository of concepts, principles, rhetoric and tradition common to all political contenders.'[51]

'New Unionism'?

Whilst the Liberal Unionist and Conservative Associations in the burgh merged in 1908 to form the Paisley Unionist Association – four years before the national bodies united as the Scottish Unionist Association – it was clear that the creation of the new joint body did not herald the resolution of the ambiguities inherent in the Unionist identity. Confusion was still apparent when in 1908 the burgh's new Unionist candidate, Captain Duncan Campbell, attempted to sum up the ideals of the new party:

> the ideals of the old Conservative Party and the Liberal Unionist party were practically the same, for did they not realise that the Unionist Party of today largely embraced the Liberal principles of many years ago prior to the great mistakes the Liberals made in 1885? Did they not realise that the Liberal Unionists were simply what they might call the more progressive members of the great Unionist Party? [52]

As late as 1908, two political traditions continued to seek accommodation in a vision as yet unclear and in an identity still contested.

Moffat's legacy to the party – an emphasis on working class support and social reform – was, however, significant in pointing a way forward. The Unionist candidates of the 1890s had earlier integrated social reforms into their addresses which, without them, would have otherwise been rather hollow testaments of faith in a Unionist status quo with little bearing on domestic issues. In his address to the Paisley electorate in 1892, for example, the Unionist candidate, Christopher N. Johnston, maintained that he was in favour of

> the simplification of the Transfer of Land, Greater facilities for the Acquirement of Land for Public Purposes and Dwelling Homes, the Abolition of Primogeniture and Entail, Popular Control of the Drink Traffic, State Aid to Insurance against Old Age, Amendment of the Law of Employers' Liability, Reform of the Poor Laws and of Parochial Administration, the Extension of the Factory Acts, with Special Provisions against sweating, and the Prohibition of Pauper Immigration from Abroad.[53]

He concluded: 'The issue before the country is clear – an era of continued social reform or a new chapter of civil strife.'

Three years later, Alexander Moffatt repeated this programme, adding commitments to a reform of the House of Lords, support for many measures to check intemperance, a promise to extend land rights and land availability in Scotland and a pledge in favour of Boards of Conciliation in industrial disputes.[54] A great many of Moffatt's addresses in 1895 were concerned specifically with labour issues, and although losing the election of that year to the sitting Liberal member, the Unionist vote increased substantially.[55] Following John Moffat's resignation in 1905, therefore, local precedents existed for the continued successful integration of social reform within the Unionist programme.

In January 1906, George H. Coats announced to a crowded Town Hall meeting that 'the real Radical Party, in the genuine and splendid sense of the word, was not the party of the Liberals, but the party of the Unionists'.[56] In the subsequent election, three candidates sought 'the weaver vote': the Liberal, John M. McCallum; the Unionist, J. A. D. McKean and for Labour, Robert Smillie. Each drew on a different strand of the Radical thread. Yet, though McCallum's victory highlighted Paisley's continued commitment to the Liberal Party, his opponents' campaigns indicated the growing popularity of political alternatives. The *Paisley and Renfrewshire Gazette* remarked that at the height of the campaign, of the 'brilliant colours and striking drawings (posted on hoardings) to arrest the attention . . . all, or nearly all . . . seem to advertise the Unionist and Labour candidates' claims for support.'[57] MacKean also called on the services of the 'First Division of the Light Brigade' – a Unionist working class propaganda machine which conducted open air meetings and delivered 'shirt sleeve orations' on 'Current Politics from the Tory Working Man's Standpoint'.[58] The 'Division' attracted large crowds, but failed to undermine the political capital in Free Trade at this election which saw the Liberals returned to power with a dramatic majority.

Four years later, however, Captain Duncan Campbell, the latest Unionist challenger, was more successful. Having been adopted by the local party in 1908, Campbell immediately styled Unionist propaganda in the burgh as the defence of working class interests and the only guarantee of social reform. Campbell's strategy echoed that of John Moffat before him. In the run up to the election of January 1910, he observed:

many of our old businesses were going to the wall, and unemployment was the great evil of our time. Why? because the foreigner was not taxed, and because our own industries were taxed by our own government.[59]

Yet Campbell went one step further. Replying to a questionnaire issued by the Paisley Trades Council, Campbell announced that he 'recognised the principle of the right to work'[60], and earned himself the endorsement of *Forward* in an article which styled Paisley's Liberal MP as a 'notorious reactionary'. Although his response did not endear Campbell to some local Unionists, who considered it 'the very height of Socialism', his position on the 'Right to Work' question reflects the extent to which Campbell stretched the conventional parameters of party politics and tested the 'traditional' Liberal vote of the burgh.[62]

The 'traditional vote' was tested again less than twelve months later when a second general election was called in December. On 26th November, the Unionists adopted their new 'champion': A. R. Jephcott, a native of Birmingham, well-known trade unionist in the Amalgamated Society of Engineers, President of the Birmingham Trades Council between 1889 and 1891 and local councillor for the largest Birmingham ward since 1895. He became Paisley's 'Working Man Unionist Candidate'.[63]

Jephcott's programme echoed the interests of Moffat and Campbell and the social reform focus of Paisley Unionism in the 1890s. Most importantly, however, he continued the tradition of reaffirming Unionism's Radical inheritance and rhetoric. In his campaign literature, capitalisation and bold face lettering isolated the essential distinctions between Unionism and the Liberal Party, which, standing juxtaposed, gained meaning through comparison with their apparent opposite. Liberalism was made to stand on its head as words became the site of the political battle. (See Appendix 4.2)

Again, however, the Unionists were defeated and again the Beaconsfield Club President blamed the 'traditional vote':

he was of opinion that if the majority of the working people had got rid of their *inherited politics*, they would have supported their fellow workman, Mr Jephcott.[64]

It was clear by 1910 that both Liberals and Unionists had come to rely on alternative definitions of the burgh's Radical Tradition to distinguish themselves as the 'truer' guardians of the town's political identity. Liberalism, however, proved most adept at gauging the extent to which that tradition could be tested whilst still preserving its meaning, its electoral potential, and – to borrow Lawrence's phrase – its 'mobilising ability'.[65]

Conclusion

In December 1911, Harry Mehan, the Unionist candidate for West Renfrewshire, addressed a demonstration of Paisley Unionists.

> It occurred to him . . . that if some of the Paisley folk's worthy ancestors were to rise from their graves and see what their descendants called Radicalism or Liberalism, they would have something to say about it. In his opinion, the only thing remaining of the good old Liberalism as they all knew it, and respected it, were a few faded portraits of the late Mr Gladstone.[66]

The contradictory tendencies in Paisley's Radical Tradition and the uneasy alliances which Gladstonian Liberalism had contained until 1886 soon asserted themselves when the Home Rule crisis brought them to light. Yet, on abandoning the Liberal Party, Liberal Unionists did not necessarily abandon its Radical heritage and took many of its principles with them into the new Unionist alliance. As the heritage of a new doctrine, what mattered was the criticism to which the Radical Tradition was subjected by the new party and the extent to which it would remain the principle object of the old. It was through this dual process of association and differentiation and the different relative weighting which each party came to place on its components that identities would be reformed. What had been secondary, subordinate or even incidental in the Liberal interpretation of Radicalism became the major features of Unionism's claim to the Radical inheritance.[67]

The Liberal Party's more successful encapsulation of Radical principles was neither inevitable nor 'natural', but was contingent on a number of factors outwith the scope of this study. The initial absence and early weakness of a party expounding the more extreme tenets of Paisley Radicalism; the continued economic health of the burgh; the strength of local industrial paternalism – all of these were significant. Yet it was only through public and private interpretations of material changes – interpretations ultimately bound by language – that the meaning of experience could be appreciated. Change does not simply happen, what is important is the way that it is understood and historically shaped by precedent, locality and tradition.

NOTES

1. George Eliot, *Felix Holt, The Radical*, F.C. Thomson (ed.) (Oxford, 1988 Edition), Ch. 2. (My italics.) F. C. Thomson has suggested that Eliot began the novel in March 1865 without a clear chronological and political framework for the piece and that it was not until five months into the writing process that Eliot focussed on the 1832 election campaign.

2. This perspective is influenced by Gramsci's formulation that 'the philosophy of an historical epoch is . . . nothing other than the history of that epoch itself, nothing other than the mass of variations that the leading group has succeeded in imposing on preceding reality'. (Antonio Gramsci, (trans. Q. Hoare & G. N. Smith), *Selections from the Prison Notebooks* (London, 1971), p. 345.

3. The work of many authors adopting post-structuralist perspectives in the writing of history has been influential in the writing of this piece, notably: J. W. Scott *Gender and the Politics of History* (Columbia, 1988); P. Joyce, *Visions of the People: Industrial England and the Question of Class 1840–1914* (Cambridge, 1991), *Democratic Subjects: The self and the social in nineteenth century England* (Cambridge, 1994).

4. R. Turner, 'Gala Day as an Expression of Community Identity', in A. Jackson (ed.), *Way of Life and Identity*, (SSRC, NSDOP Occasional Paper No. 4, 1981), p. 63. See also: D. B. Clark, 'The Concept of Community: A Re-examination', *The Sociological Review*, 21 (1973), pp. 397–416 and C. J. Calhoun, 'Community: Toward a Variable Conceptualization for Comparable Research', *Social History* 5 (1980), pp. 105–127.

5. A. Dickson and W. Speirs, 'Changes in Class Structure in Paisley, 1750–1845', *Scottish Historical Review*, 59 (1980), pp. 54–72; A. Dickson and A. Clarke, 'Class Consciousness in Early Industrial Capitalism: Paisley 1770–1850', in A. Dickson (ed.) *Capital and Class in Scotland* (Edinburgh, 1982), pp. 8–60, also 'Social Concern and Social Control in Nineteenth Century Scotland: Paisley 1841–1843', *Scottish Historical Review*, 65 (1986), pp. 48–60.

6. Clarke and Dickson, 'Social Concern and Social Control', pp. 55–56.

7. See R. Brown, *The History of Paisley from the Roman Period to 1884* (Paisley, 1886), pp. 424–427.

8. Clarke and Dickson, 'Social Concern and Social Control', p. 57.

9. Dickson and Clarke, 'Class Consciousness in Early Industrial Capitalism', p. 53.

10. M. McCarthy, *A Social Geography of Paisley* (Paisley, 1969), p. 162.

11. Joyce, *Visions*, p. 77.

12. See W. W. Knox 'The Political and Workplace Culture of the Scottish Working Class, 1832–1914', in W. H. Fraser and R. J. Morris (eds) *People and Society in Scotland*, Vol. II, 1830–1914 (Edinburgh, 1990), pp. 138–167; *Hanging By a Thread: The Scottish Cotton Industry, c.1850–1914* (Preston, 1995).

13. A. Warde, 'Spatial Change, Politics and the Division of Labour', in D. Gregory and J. Urry (eds), *Social Relations and Spatial Structures* (Basingstoke, 1985), p. 165.
14. Calhoun, 'Community: toward a variable conceptualisation', p. 116.
15. J. W. Scott, 'The Evidence of Experience', *Critical Inquiry*, (1991), pp. 792–793. See, for example, L. Wright, Scottish Chartism (Edinburgh, 1953), p. 103;
16. D. Howell, *British Workers and the Independent Labour Party 1888–1906* (Manchester, 1983), p. 143.
17. Joyce, *Visions*, p. 77.
18. R. Williams, *Keywords: A Vocabulary of Culture and Society* (London, 1983), p. 22.
19. Graham Goodlad, 'Gladstone and His Rivals: Popular Liberal Perceptions of the Party Leadership in the Political Crisis of 1885–6', in E. F. Biagini and A. J. Reid (eds), *Currents of Radicalism* (Cambridge, 1991), pp. 163–164.
20. A. J. Lee, 'Conservatism, Traditionalism and the British Working Class, 1880–1918', in D. E. Martin and D. Rubinstein (eds), *Ideology and the Labour Movement* (London, 1979), p. 98.
21. *Paisley and Renfrewshire Gazette*, 1 May 1886.
22. Note: Aside from the Ayr Association, the Paisley Liberal and Radical Unionist Association was the only branch of the West of Scotland Liberal Unionist Association (WSLUA) to stress its Radical roots in its title.
23. *Paisley Chronicle*, 26 Jun. 1886.
24. John McCaffrey emphasises that Liberal split involved 'the Gladstonians enjoying the support of the labouring masses as the Liberal Unionists drew closer in practice and spirit to the Conservatives'. 'The Origins of Liberal Unionism in the West of Scotland', *Scottish Historical Review* 50 (1971), p. 71.
25. *Paisley and Renfrewshire Gazette*, 16 April 1887.
26. *Paisley Daily Express*, 24 June 1886. (My italics.)
27. *Paisley Daily Express*, 29 June 1886. (My italics.)
28. *Paisley Chronicle*, 12 June 1886. (My italics.)
29. *Paisley and Renfrewshire Gazette*, 19 Nov. 1887.
30. *Paisley and Renfrewshire Gazette*, 27 Dec. 1890.
31. *Paisley and Renfrewshire Gazette*, 21 April 1894.
32. *Paisley and Renfrewshire Gazette*, 28 April 1894. (My italics.)
33. See P. Brewster (Rev.), *His Chartist and Socialist Sermons* (Glasgow, 1910)
34. C. M. M. Macdonald, 'The Radical Thread: Political Change in Scotland, Paisley Politics 1885–1924', (Unpublished PhD Thesis, University of Strathclyde, 1996), p. 74.
35. J. Lawrence, 'Class and Gender in the Making of Urban Toryism, 1880–1914', *English Historical Review*, 108 (1993), p. 634.
36. M. Fforde, *Collectivism and Conservatism, 1886–1914*, (Edinburgh, 1990), p. 88.
37. E. H. H. Green, 'Radical Conservatism: The Electoral Genesis of Tariff Reform', *Historical Journal*, 28 (1985), p. 686.
38. Strathclyde Regional Archives, Parker Smith Collection, TD1.46, 'Cuttings', (Various).
39. N[ational] L[ibrary] of S[cotland], S[cottish] C[onservative and] U[nionist] A[ssociation] MSS, Acc. 10424/21, WSLUA Minutes 1900–1910, Business

Committee Meeting, 10 June 1903; Business Committee Meeting 30 Oct. 1903; Annual General Meeting, 3 Dec. 1903; Executive Committee Meeting, 9 Dec. 1903.

40. NLS, SCUA MSS, Acc. 10424/21, WSLUA Minutes 1900–1910, Annual General Meeting, 23 Nov. 1904.
41. *Paisley Daily Express*, 30 Dec. 1905.
42. Ramsay MacDonald commented on this strategy of Tariff Reformers: '(Chamberlain) attempted to found a *prima facie* argument that Trade Unionists ought to be Protectionists on the superficial resemblance between the two movements. But even when the Trade Unionist could not argue the difference, he *felt* the difference and remained unconvinced.' J. R. MacDonald, 'Mr Chamberlain as a Social Reformer', Rt. Hon. Viscount Milner et. al., *Life of Joseph Chamberlain* (London, c.1914), p. 191 (My italics.)
43. J. Lawrence, 'Popular Politics and the Limitations of Party: Wolverhampton, 1867–1900', Biagini and Reid (eds) *Currents of Radicalism*, p. 75.
44. *Paisley Daily Express*, 27 Dec. 1907.
45. *Paisley Daily Express*, 7 Dec. 1904.
46. As quoted in *Paisley Daily Express*, 6 Feb. 1905.
47. *Paisley Daily Express*, 3 May 1905.
48. *Paisley and Renfrewshire Gazette*, 17 June 1905; *Paisley Daily Express*, 16 June 1905.
49. *Paisley Daily Express*, 5 Dec. 1905. (From a letter from Moffat to the press dated 18 May 1905.)
50. Macdonald, 'The Radical Thread', p. 168.
51. *Ibid.*, p. 168.
52. *Paisley and Renfrewshire Gazette*, 17 Oct. 1908.
53. *Paisley Daily Express*, 27 June 1892.
54. *Paisley and Renfrewshire Gazette*, 6 July 1895.
55. See Appendix 4.1.
56. *Paisley and Renfrewshire Gazette*, 6 Jan. 1906.
57. *Paisley and Renfrewshire Gazette*, 13 Jan. 1906.
58. *Paisley and Renfrewshire Gazette*, 5 Jan. 1906.
59. *Paisley and Renfrewshire Gazette*, 25 Dec. 1909.
60. *Paisley Daily Express*, 10 Jan. 1910.
61. *Forward*, 14 Jan. 1910.
62. The President of the Beaconsfield Club emphasised Campbell's popularity in the face of reactionary Liberalism: 'there was many a man present who would have voted for Captain Campbell, but who was still chained to his old traditional vote'. (*Paisley and Renfrewshire Gazette*, 22 Jan. 1910.)
63. *Paisley and Renfrewshire Gazette*, 3 Dec. 1910.
64. *Paisley and Renfrewshire Gazette*, 10 Dec. 1910. (My italics.)
65. Lawrence, 'Class and Gender in the Making of Urban Toryism', p. 634.
66. *Paisley and Renfrewshire Gazette*, 9 Dec. 1911.
67. Gramsci, *Selections from the Prison Notebooks*, p. 195.

APPENDIX

4.1 Paisley Parliamentary Election Results, 1885–1910

Election	Electors	Turn-out	Candidate	Party	Votes	%
1885	6,794	87.0	W. B. Barbour	Lib	3,390	57.3
			R. M. McKerrell	Con	2,523	42.7
					867	*14.6*
1886	6,794	81.7	W. B. Barbour	Lib	3,057	55.1
			J. P. Smith	L.U.	2,491	44.9
					566	*10.2*
(DEATH)						
1891	8,107	85.8	W. Dunn	Lib	4,145	59.6
(1/6)			R. M. McKerrell	Con	2,807	40.4
					1,338	*19.2*
1892	8,223	81.5	W. Dunn	Lib	4,262	63.6
			C. N. Johnston	Con	2,441	36.4
					1,821	*27.2*
1895	9,105	82.0	Sir W. Dunn Bt.	Lib	4,404	59.0
			A. Moffatt	Con	3,062	41.0
					1,342	*18.0*
1900	10,758	74.4	Sir W. Dunn Bt.	Lib	4,532	56.6
			G. S. C. Swinton	Con	3,474	43.4
					1,058	*13.2*
1906	12,179	88.2	J. M. McCallum	Lib	5,664	52.7
			J. A. D. McKean	L. U.	2,594	24.2
			R. Smillie	SWRC	2,482	23.1
					3,070	*28.5*
1910 (J)	12,331	86.8	J. M. McCallum	Lib	6,812	63.7
			D. F. Campbell	Con	3,890	36.3
					2,922	*27.4*
1910 (D)	12,541	74.9	J. M. McCallum	Lib	6,039	64.3
			A. R. Jephcott	Con	3,350	35.7
					2,689	*28.6*

SOURCE: F. W. S. Craig, *British Parliamentary Elections 1885–1918* (London, 1974), Table 494, p. 517.

4.2 *Unionist Campaign Literature, 1910*

(1)   The **LIBERAL** Policy would **MAINTAIN THE HEREDITARY PRINCIPLE** in the House of Lords.

The **UNIONIST** Policy would **ABOLISH THAT HEREDITARY PRINCIPLE.**

(2)   The **LIBERAL** Policy would introduce **SINGLE CHAMBER GOVERN-MENT.**

The **UNIONIST** Policy would maintain an **ELECTED SECOND CHAMBER** to prevent hasty and ill-considered legislation.

(3)   The **LIBERAL** Policy would enable a temporary **COALITION of MINORI-TIES,** such as now exists, to over-ride the will of the people.

The **UNIONIST** Policy would not allow a **REAL MAJORITY** of the people to be dominated by a temporary combination of minorities.

(4)   The **LIBERAL** Party is **AFRAID** to trust the people with the **REFEREN-DUM.**

The **UNIONIST** Party recognises the **SOVEREIGN WILL** of the **PEOPLE** through the **REFERENDUM.**

(5)   The **LIBERAL** Policy would make the **Party Leaders** the **Masters** of the People.

The **UNIONIST** Policy would make the **PEOPLE** their own **MASTERS.**

(6)   The **LIBERAL** Policy would give **HOME RULE** to **IRELAND** without further reference to the People.

The **Unionist** Policy would insist that Home Rule be definitely decided by the **People's Referendum.**

(7)   **THE LIBERAL POLICY is calculated to destroy the Freedom of the People.**

THE UNIONIST POLICY would give them absolute control over the affairs of the Nation.

SOURCE: *Paisley and Renfrewshire Gazette*, 3 Dec. 1910.

5

SCOTTISH UNIONISM BETWEEN THE TWO WORLD WARS

I. G. C. Hutchinson

The Electoral Record

The electoral record of the Scottish Unionist Party between the wars was impressive, viewed historically. Before 1918, the Conservative/ Unionist interest had been the largest party in Scotland in only one general election out of twenty held since the 1832 Reform Act. Of the fifteen held since the Second World War, they have secured a majority of Scottish seats on only one occasion. By comparison, in four of the seven inter-war general elections, the Tories had the most MPs. The party was not just the beneficiary of the electoral roulette which prevailed in this era. The Unionist share of the poll in Scotland grew steadily between the elections of 1922 and 1935, suggesting that significant advances were being logged. Initially Scotland lagged well behind England, but by the last contest before the war, the gap had narrowed appreciably. The contrast with Wales is instructive. There the Tories never achieved any comparable momentum, their share of the vote remaining virtually static over the period. The consequence was that while at the start of the era, Wales and Scotland were closer to each other than to England in terms of Conservative support, by the end Scotland had moved nearer to England, leaving Wales as the isolated case. (Appendix, Tables 5.1 & 5.2)

This achievement created a sense of confidence among Scottish Tories, underlined both by the calibre of the party's MPs and also by their readiness to articulate their political ideas. It became a commonplace after the Second World War that Scottish Tory MPs were of such poor quality that apart from the obligation to have one as Scottish Secretary, none were fit for Cabinet rank. From 1951 until 1986, when the party was in office for a total of twenty-five years, no

Scottish MP held any other Cabinet post, with the anomalous exception of Sir Alec Douglas-Home, who became a Scottish member after he had been chosen for the premiership. Between 1918 and 1939, however, when the Tories were in office (either solely or in coalition) for eighteen years, Scottish MPs in the Cabinet included one Prime Minister (Bonar Law), one Chancellor of the Exchequer (R.S. Horne), one Home Secretary (Sir John Gilmour), two Agriculture Ministers (Gilmour and W. Elliot) and one Health Secretary (Elliot).

Several of the Scottish parliamentary party were able exponents of the Conservative cause, using different media with equal facility. Their contributions, moreover, were central to the statement of Conservative principles in a British context: their arguments carried resonance furth of Scotland. Noel Skelton is widely credited with having coined one of the most seminal phrases in twentieth-century Conservatism: 'a property-owning democracy'.[1] The Duchess of Atholl produced the influential *Women and Politics*, which tried to convey why British women should support the Conservatives.[2] A third Scot who had an audience throughout Great Britain was Walter Elliot. He was an inveterate writer of newspaper articles for both the London and the Scottish press. In 1927 he wrote a book on Conservatism, as part of a series of books designed to state the right-wing viewpoint on contemporary politics.[3] That Elliott should be invited to define the central theme of the whole series indicates the weight he carried.[4]

The Scottish MPs were also strong debaters, both within the Commons and outside. Boothby and Atholl were excellent orators whether on the stump or in parliament, and R. S. Horne in his heyday was another well-regarded performer. These speakers were all in regular demand to put the party's case to the public. The most impressive spokesman was probably Elliot, who had been a star debater in his student days at Glasgow University. So secure was Elliot that he attended an ILP Summer School in 1930 to debate political topics with the socialists.[5]

Party Organisation

Organisation was, both at the time and in the view of historians, one of the key factors in Conservative success. In contrast to Liberal and Labour, the Tories appeared dynamic and efficient. The party set itself a goal of having organisers in every constituency, and by 1927 only eleven of the 71 seats were without a full-time organiser.[6] The amount of literature distributed was mountainous: in the run-up to the 1929 general election, five million leaflets were delivered in the western half of Scotland alone.[7] The party produced free newspapers to reach voters: in 1938, 370,000 copies of the *Scottish Illustrated* were sent out in the western area.[8] A huge number of meetings were held to preach the party message: in 1926–7, nearly 2,500 took place – about 45 each week.[9]

The party showed great versatility in approaching organisational questions, adjusting flexibly to changing social conditions. By the end of the 1920s a groundswell of opinion indicated that some key elements of the traditional format of grass-roots campaigning, notably public meetings – even with prominent speakers – and literature distribution, were losing their impact: 'Modern conditions call for modern methods of treatment: it is becoming increasingly difficult to secure the interest or attention of electors along former lines of procedure.'[10]

The cinema vans, launched in 1930, were a skilful innovation, shrewdly blending general interest with a modicum of palatable politicking. A typical programme, offered in 1938, consisted of: 'Heritage of Industry' (including footage of factories 'running to full capacity'), 'Heritage of Defence', some cartoons and a short address by the Prime Minister.[11] The vans did yeoman service, particularly in out-of-the-way localities and in areas of unemployment and poverty, where a free evening's entertainment was an irresistible lure. They drew large audiences: 3,000 in a single year were said to have attended showings in one constituency alone.[12] Equally importantly, the vans caught a different audience to the Unionist faithful: 'A feature of these meetings is the opportunity they provide for members and prospective candidates to reach a section of the electorate not readily attracted to the more ordinary political gatherings.'[13]

The party's news-sheets changed: the *Scottish Unionist* had folded by 1930, due to dwindling interest.[14] It was replaced in 1935 by the *Scottish Illustrated*, a title significantly devoid of overt political content, and designed to reach a wider audience by using attractive pictures.[15] Sweeping changes were made to leaflets, after complaints that literature issued from London did not always reflect Scottish conditions and priorities. The Scottish Whip's Office undertook to produce material of specifically Scottish relevance, and these were well received, notably an early pamphlet on Scottish nationalism.[16] Another innovation was the wayside posters, begun in 1938 and again targeted at a wide audience, 'focussing public notice on one given point of topical importance each month.'[17]

To boost interest, social events were given increased prominence. In 1937, St Rollox Tories held fourteen political but 28 social meetings.[18] The Kelvingrove association proudly emphasised the role of afternoon bridge and whist drive sessions in the Albert Palais de Dance and the Norwood Hotel in enticing into the party 'many people not previously interested in our work'.[19] Fetes became regular features: in 1932, there were nine in the western area alone, with up to 20,000 showing up. A prominent politician would deliver a speech – e.g., Baldwin spoke at Coltness in 1935 – and an astute mix of political indoctrination and leisure pursuits was achieved. In addition, there was an opportunity for mixing with social superiors, which was attractive to middle-class adherents. Coach trips became a feature: St Rollox Unionists went to Blackpool, while the more sedate Maryhill Tories travelled to Luss and Aberfoyle.[20]

With low attendance at meetings, greater stress was put on canvassing work, as house-to-house visiting was deemed vital in an age of mass democracy.[21] An internal post-mortem on the 1929 general election complained about the lack of door-step work, and a guide to canvassing technique was issued by party headquarters in 1935:

> It was pointed out that a detailed knowledge of politics was not so essential as the ability to explain agreeably the real purpose of the call – namely that a visit was being paid on behalf of the candidate, that an invitation to attend his or her meeting was being given and that above all the electorate should go to the polls on the election day and record his or her vote for the candidate, and that most interesting pamphlets explanatory of Government policy were available for the asking.[22]

The two master strokes of Unionist organisation, however, lay in their mobilisation of women and young people. In both departments they were far more successful than either of their rivals.

The challenges posed by the advent of a female electorate were approached from two angles. One approach was obviously to persuade women to vote Unionist, and the other was to recruit them into the party and then train them to be effective workers for the cause. Great emphasis was placed on displaying visibly the place of women in the party. Each constituency association was instructed to have a woman as one to its two vice-presidents. The first woman Scottish MP (Duchess of Atholl) was a Tory, and throughout the inter-war years the party's record in this respect was superior to its competitors. Not only did three women sit as Tories, against two Labour and no Liberal, but they served for longer periods: a combined total of 29 years, against Labour's four.[23] The Unionist record on women candidatures in inter-war general elections was better too, at sixteen, compared to twelve Labour and six Liberal. The party's electoral message was also heavily tilted towards issues seen as of particular concern to women, as is discussed below.

Within the party, women's sections were enthusiastically developed. By 1924, 200 women's committees had been set up in the eastern area alone.[24] Four women organisers were in post by 1926, charged with stimulating membership and activities.[25] A vast number of meetings for women were held annually – around 800 in 1926–7 – either by the paid organisers or by party members.[26] For the committed, lecture courses were held on current affairs, constitutional theory and practice and topical questions of the day. Thus in 1932 a series of talks on political history was run in Glasgow, while in Edinburgh some six years later, discussion groups considered food prices, the Pensions Act and the Gilmour report on Scottish government.[27] These events were well attended: 325 came to a lecture programme by Irene Ward in 1926; and 150 and eighty were present at talks in Glasgow that same year on, respectively, housing and economics.[28] Day and weekend schools also served to deepen members' knowledge of politics, and again these were well patronised: 400 showed up for an Edinburgh day conference in 1935.[29] These were seen as having an 'infectious' impact, as other women were 'awakened to the importance of acquiring a working knowledge of the political questions of the day.'[30]

Speakers' classes were organised regularly from the later 1920s to help women acquire greater political competence.[31] During the 1923 general election, instruction in canvassing was offered and proved very popular.[32] A special feature was the holding of kitchen and garden meetings to spread party propaganda in intimate surroundings: these were held to be highly effective, for instance, during the 1924 Kelvingrove by-election.[33] The success of these schemes was attested in 1924, when it was reported that:

> The women are indefatigable in taking their share of organisation and propaganda and in acquiring a knowledge of politics, and are showing much less diffidence than formerly in standing alongside the men in Party warfare.[34]

In addition to standard electioneering work, women devoted their efforts to boosting the finances of the party. Whist drives were a favourite device: one whist and bridge drive drew 662 players and raised £140.[35] Another field of activity was organising fetes and bazaars.

The Junior Imperial League was revived in Scotland after the First World War to reach those between fifteen and twenty-five years of age. By the end of the 1920s it had some 20,000 members in nearly 250 branches, covering most constituencies.[36] Its role was defined by the Scottish Unionist Association as being to create a body of informed opinion among the young on Unionist principles; to recruit into the senior organisation; and to render assistance in ordinary political circumstances and also at elections.[37]

Each of these goals was pretty well met. There was indeed a fair measure of social activity, such as golf and tennis competitions. But increasingly after about 1930, these more frivolous pursuits were supplanted by straight political work. In 1931 1,000 meetings were held in the western area alone.[38] Some branches had their own libraries, and in the west of Scotland there was a debating competition.[39] Study schools were held regularly to inculcate a knowledge of Unionist principles and policies.[40] The League was allotted an active role at the Scottish Unionist Association annual conference, which in 1938 was extended over two days in order to create time for resolutions submitted by league branches to be fully discussed.[41] The advantage of having the league as a conduit into the adult association was emphasised by the election of two league members to Glasgow City Council in 1936.[42] Electioneering was a strong facet of league work. In the 1935 general election members were deployed in canvassing and carrying out clerical duties in many seats.[43]

The Young Unionists (whose alternative name, Young Britons, seems to have been used interchangeably) were a further refinement of the Unionist youth policy, designed for eight to fifteen year-olds. The first branch appears to have been started in Bridgeton in 1923, and soon had 600 enrolled.[44] The movement spread through the western areas in particular in the rest of the inter-war years. In 1935 three Glasgow constituencies had between 150 and 220 Young Unionists and a comparable number of Junior Imperialists.[45] Not much overt political activity went on at the weekly meetings, where a short address was accompanied by musical and other entertainment. The only significant political indoctrination came on Empire Day: Glasgow members (numbering between 400 and 600 in the thirties) marched in procession to a service at the Cenotaph.[46] Otherwise, the emphasis was on entertainment: a Young Unionist choir was formed in 1932, and held annual choral concerts, as well as performing at constituencies' social occasions.[47]

While there is considerable force in the claim that superior organisation gave the Tories a major advantage, it should not be taken too far. The failure of the news-sheets and the relative lateness, in the 1930s, of these new initiatives in propaganda technique suggest that they had a limited impact in this era. There was also the constant reforming of political education programmes for party workers: one scheme was started in 1926–8, but by the mid-1930s efforts were again made to start up these groups.[48] In 1936 it was agreed that 'pivotal' party workers should be politically knowledgeable.[49] This might suggest a high turnover of members, low commitment, or a stunted level of political awareness. A pointer to the frail nature of political awareness possessed by even committed party members was made in 1934. Worries were expressed about the approach adopted at the party's training college, Ashridge, where all sides of political arguments were presented. This, it was claimed, had the unfortunate result of 'confusing' participants.[50]

Again, on closer inspection, the professional organisers seem rather unimpressive. Unlike their English equivalents, the Scottish agents spent a great deal of time in routine office work and in fundraising to meet their own salary and expenses. As a consequence, limited time was spent on actually improving organisation.[51] The English agents' association declined to recognise Scottish organisers as fully trained, so it was difficult for Scots to get posts in England.[52] Moreover, the appointment of an organiser was not a necessary prerequisite for political success: Cathcart Unionists managed to retain the seat from 1922 despite not having a paid organiser until 1926.[53]

The financial basis of organisational supremacy also needs some qualification. In 1924 subscriptions had still not regained their pre-1914 levels.[54] Given the extensive inflation that occurred over that decade, in real terms the party was clearly much poorer. Moreover, the maximum inter-war annual income – £17,974 – was reached in 1929. Throughout the 1930s income never rose above two thirds of that figure; indeed in 1933–4 it was exactly one half.[55] So serious was the financial crisis that in 1931 some of the central office staff were dismissed and the pay of many of those surviving the purge was cut by 10 per cent.[56] Even as late as 1939 the Western Divisional Council was financially embarrassed to the extent of £500.[57] Many local parties were also in straitened circumstances: several dispensed with their paid organisers in 1931–2.[58] Cathcart was burdened with a deficit for most of the 1930s, and was still £141 in the red on the eve of war.[59] Yet it was in the 1930s, when the Tories were badly strapped for cash, that the main electoral advances were made.

The size and quality of membership are problematic. In 1931 the membership of the Glasgow Unionist Association numbered about 30,000. This figure probably exceeded the entire individual member-ship of the Labour Party in Scotland. Yet these statistics may be mis-leading. In 1932–3 the Cathcart Unionists discovered that inflated membership statistics had been compiled by the former secretary of the association. In lieu of the previously claimed 2,408 members, the true paid-up tally came to between 500 and 600. The balance were either dead, or had moved away, while branches alleged to be active proved to exist in name only.[60] This may be part of a campaign of denigration designed to discredit the outgoing officer, but if true and representative, this would suggest a real membership across the city of perhaps 10,000. A large paper membership, moreover, did not necessarily denote high levels of activism. It is unclear how many of those playing bridge under the auspices of the Kelvingrove associa-tion actually canvassed the tenements during elections.

The relevance of organisation to electoral victory can also be doubted from the evidence of constituencies like West Aberdeenshire. Here the Tories seized a seat in 1923 which had been Liberal for over a generation, and then retained it virtually without effort thereafter. Yet at the time of the gain, the party had no proper organisation on the ground, and put up a candidate only after the general election campaign had begun, because it was initially felt that the prospects of victory were slender.[61]

The Politics of Scotland's National Institutions

If organisation can at best be counted a partial success, the reasons for the positive achievements of the Unionists may be identified elsewhere. Two possible foci of attention present themselves. One is the manner in which Conservatism became identified with key aspects of Scottish national institutions. Linked to this are changes in the political culture which removed some of the policy disabilities under which the party had hitherto laboured. A second approach is to emphasise the policies espoused by the party, which neatly yoked anti-socialism to a strong amount of progressive ideas.

A major feature of this period was that the main pillars of Scottish civil society were overwhelmingly well-disposed towards Conservatism. This had not been the case between 1832 and 1914, and it was the gradual distancing of these institutions from the 1960s which contributed to the Conservatives' decline.

Before 1914, the morning newspapers in the main cities were in roughly partisan equipoise. From the mid-1920s these organs were uniformly Tory. Mergers between the two dailies in both Dundee and Aberdeen wiped out the Liberal organ in each city; the Glasgow-based Liberal *Daily Record* was switched to new owners (the Berry brothers) and joined the Unionist camp; and the *Glasgow Herald* and the *Scotsman*, of course, remained firmly Unionist over this period. In addition, the *Bulletin*, launched in Glasgow in 1915, was broadly Unionist, as befitted a stable-mate to the *Herald*. The Scots proved pretty impervious to penetration by the metropolitan daily press throughout these years. Only the mostly pro-Conservative *Scottish Daily Express*, begun in 1928, managed successfully to break into the Scottish market. Labour's *Daily Herald* and the Liberal *News Chronicle*, by contrast, seem to have had a minimal impact.

The Unionist hegemony was reinforced by additions and dilutions to the Scottish press in this period. The arrival in 1919 of the *Sunday Post* and the *Sunday Mail* added two Unionist papers, both with very heavy market saturation.[62] On the other hand, the Liberal *People's Journal* was transmogrified under new ownership from a powerful pre-war radical weekly feared by Tories into a 'twee' blend of Kailyard, kitsch and knitting patterns.[63] The Liberals had lost one of their most potent voices.

At the less exalted level of the local press, the advantage during the inter-war years swung equally heavily towards the Unionists. Before the First World War it was customary for most towns and rural areas to possess journals representing each side of the political divide. As Table 5.3 (Appendix) reveals, over a quarter of a century the bias of the press altered decisively.

It must be borne in mind that these statistics seriously understate the Unionist weight. In both years, for instance, the *Glasgow Herald* and the *Dundee Courier* did not indicate any party affiliations. While those professing Unionist beliefs shrank between 1913 and 1938, the Liberal press was effectively annihilated. The consequence was that the Unionist papers had a fairly free run in most parts of the country. The only two papers of any substance still Liberal in 1938 were the *Greenock Telegraph* and the *Paisley Daily Express*. It may be no coincidence that these were virtually the only large industrial constituencies where the Liberals were successful between the wars.

Further sustenance for the Tories came from changes in the presbyterian churches. The stream of church mergers set in train in 1900 had two beneficial aspects for the Tories. Firstly, the progression towards full presbyterian union (achieved in 1929) meant that old grievances of the non-state churches, such as disestablishment, were no longer aired. It had been these issues which had disposed dissenting presbyterians towards Liberalism before 1914.

The second factor was that after 1918, the Church of Scotland was unequivocally Unionist. Following the reunion of 1929, any residual Liberalism associated with the United Free Church (which had in any event been much eroded by the class and political polarisation of 1914–29) was easily swamped by the larger Church of Scotland, traditionally closer to the Tories. The presbyterian churches had enthusiastically supported the First World War, offering little succour to anti-war critics. After 1918, the Church of Scotland continued to hold to its deeply anti-radical stance. Most clergymen denounced the General Strike with unrestrained vehemence.[64] The problems of unemployment and social decay in the 1930s were, by and large, ignored by the General Assembly. John White, the dominant influence in the church throughout this period, was a whole-hearted Unionist.[65] Under his regime, socially concerned individuals like George Macleod were effectively neutralised within the Church. Thus the high prestige still accorded to presbyterianism within Scottish society was helpful to the Unionists.

The legal profession, which in Scotland had always had important linkages with politics, became overwhelmingly Unionist after 1918. In the twenty years preceding 1914 eleven Liberal MPs were advocates, but only six Unionists were. Recruitment to the judiciary was thus bi-partisan: nine Liberals and four Unionists became judges or sheriffs.[66] Between the wars twenty-four advocates sat as Tory MPs, while there were two apiece for Labour and the Liberals. Only one Unionist, but both Liberals (and no Labour), had sat in the Commons before 1914. Thus ninety per cent of advocates sitting for the first time between 1918 and 1939 were Tories. So overwhelming was the bias that the first Labour administration of 1924 had to use two Tories to fill the Scottish law offices. This of course reinforced the image of the Unionists as the natural political home of the law. Most of these lawyers – in fact, fourteen of the twenty-four – moved on fairly briskly to the judicial bench, but they gave invaluable benefit to the Unionist party, by providing highly effective debaters in the Commons. Men like the future Lords Cooper, Normand and Reid were first class speakers. It is significant that in 1937 the central party managers were insistent that J.S.C. Reid be the candidate for the Hillhead vacancy, although local activists seemed disposed to look elsewhere.[67]

The Empire continued to exercise a powerful emotional and economic hold in Scotland, and the Unionists were identified very closely with it. Several Tories were appointed as colonial and dominion governors: most famously John Buchan, a Unionist MP at the time, went to Canada as governor-general in 1935.[68] Empire Day celebrations had strong Unionist overtones: in Glasgow a procession of several hundred Young Unionists would march to a service at the Cenotaph. The fractious debate among right-leaning Scottish Nationalists in the 1930s confirms the importance of Imperial sentiment.[69]

The land question, which had been a major inhibiting factor in the progress of Unionism before 1914, became less important. The break-up of many large estates after 1918 (one-fifth of the Scottish land-mass changed hands between 1918 and 1921) reduced the highly visible targets; the relative failure of post-war land resettlement projects; the changing orientation of tenant farmers as they became owner-occupiers in the 1920s; and the switch in urban areas to alternative explanations of and remedies for poor social conditions in towns – all of these helped the Unionists to soften their pre-war reactionary image.[70]

Tariff reform, another issue which had alienated large swathes of voters before 1914 because of the particular make-up of the Scottish economy, gradually lost its taboo status. In the 1923 election it still worked adversely, losing the Unionists many votes, even in the business community.[71] By 1932, however, many erstwhile free traders had dropped their opposition. The *Glasgow Herald*, hostile to protection in 1923, was stressing a decade later that the new economic circumstances required the end of laissez-faire trade policy.[72] Others, mostly Liberals, accepted that in the interests of national stability, the precepts of Adam Smith could be jettisoned.[73]

Strategies and Policies

The policy basis for the success of the Unionists between the wars reposed on two strategic foundations. On the one hand, there was the mobilisation of anti-socialist forces behind the party, using the argument that the Tories were the most reliable party to resist Labour. On the other hand, there was an appreciation that simplistic scare-mongering would not be enough on every occasion. Particular Scottish conditions influenced the latter approach, so that a progressive and socially concerned programme was deemed indispensable.

The menace of extreme socialism was, of course, a potent cry in Scotland. Images such as 'Red Clydeside'; the sizable Communist presence in some areas and industries; and the survival of the ILP in Scotland after its secession in the 1930s, were shrewdly manipulated by the Unionists with the aim of squeezing Liberals off the electoral scene. Thus in the 1918 general election, West Stirlingshire Liberals were ready to drop a century of enmity and unite with the Tories, believing that only a solid common front could defeat the challenge of the mining vote returning Tom Johnston, then seen as a dangerous revolutionary.[74]

1924 marked another high point in the anti-Socialist strategy. Liberals were excoriated for allowing a Labour administration to be formed by 'deliberate' action on their part. The disarray among Liberals was widespread and easily worked upon: a group of leading businessmen in Paisley publicly withdrew their support for Asquith and United Free Church clergymen were said to be abandoning the Liberal party in vast numbers.[75]

1931, however, represented the apogee of the politics of panic. The recurrent theme trumpeted everywhere was that Labour's incompetence, together with what the Partick Tory candidate called 'WILD EXTREMES OF NATIONALISATION AND EXTRAVAGANCE', had placed the British economy in grave peril. As a result, 'our little investments, our savings, our pensions' were in jeopardy, warned the Ayr Burghs candidate. Voters had to display a patriotism that transcended partisan feelings by repudiating Labour and the 'direct and dangerous menace which threaten the stability and safety of the State', as the Dumfries-shire candidate explained.[76] Liberals joined in this litany; one normally staunch local Liberal newspaper saying that to try socialism would be 'the very essence of madness'.[77]

Fears of Labour as a wild revolutionary movement were shrewdly targeted initially at Liberals, but also at women and a broader working class group: the Tories constantly pointed up the menace to British values which Socialism posed, especially the threat to the family. In 1931, the political dividend of the economic crisis plainly spread far beyond the middle class. The Unionists and their allies won a whole slew of working class seats, most significantly the majority of mining constituencies, as concern for jobs and prospects were paramount.

Yet this approach had its limitations. For one thing, in most of the country for most of this period Labour was not in reality extreme and even within the Scottish ILP, the Clydesiders were outvoted from about 1925 by moderates. Indeed, the secession of ILP discontents in 1932 was a confession of failure by Maxton and his associates: Labour was firmly middle of the road, and the bulk of the ILP opted to remain with Labour.

In addition, the Unionists could lose support from those who were not committed Tories if the menace of revolution was in eclipse or if they themselves appeared immoderate. The 1923 election, fought by the Tories on tariff reform, illustrated this: most Liberals voted to defend free trade, and pro-Unionist papers like the *Glasgow Herald* were also hostile.[78] Protectionism, a constituency organiser complained, 'is certain to alienate a large section of moderate opinion and thus endanger the continuation of sound constitutional government.'[79] Again in 1929, the Tories felt that they lost ground because the government was regarded in some quarters as vindictive in its handling of the miners after the strike of 1926.[80]

Accordingly, a more positive line had to operate in twin-track with anti-socialism. The key determinants of this approach were the belief that a vote for Labour was not always an expression of unwavering commitment to socialism as an ideology, and a concern lest the Liberals mount a revival. What linked these two ingredients was the Scottish social and economic context.

It was a commonplace among Liberals and Unionists throughout the period that much of the support for Labour came from pragmatic reasons and not from ideological belief, which of course suggested that such voters might be wooed away. The 1922 result in the west was interpreted by some as a protest at high unemployment and poor living conditions.[81] Sometimes, too, voting Labour was seen as an act of class solidarity rather than political conviction. One working-class Liberal pointed out the social pressures to conform to voting Labour: 'to refuse was to be stigmatised "a traitor to his class." A spirit of victimisation was then entered upon.'[82]

Liberals, in the eyes of Unionists, posed a serious electoral threat. The Scottish Tories, it must be remembered, were more concerned about the electoral threat offered by the Liberals than was the case in England. For one thing, the Liberals, although not normally getting a higher share of the poll than in England, were far more able to turn these votes into MPs. (Appendix, Table 5.4)

The menace presented by the Liberals, for the Tories, lay as much in letting Labour in as in outright defeat. This was vividly demonstrated in the 1929 election. Of the eleven seats lost by the Tories to Labour, six could be ascribed to the intervention of the Liberals where they had not stood in 1924. A further five seats were lost to the Liberals, with two partly caused by Labour standing in constituencies uncontested in 1924. Moreover, a number of seats retained by the Unionists had very narrow majorities, again due to the Liberals' increased number of candidatures. The significant impact of the Liberals was fully acknowledged by the Tories in their election post-mortem.[83]

A further factor was that the Liberals were in many seats the real alternative to the Tories, and elsewhere the Liberals remained strong in seats which the Unionists regarded as their natural terrain. Outside of a small handful of constituencies (Greenock, Leith, Montrose and Paisley), the Liberal party had virtually disappeared from urban-industrial seats by 1922–3. Their main presence thereafter was in rural or urban-residential seats. In 1929, for example, three Liberals sat for urban and ten for rural seats. Unease about the security of constituencies persisted throughout the period. As late as 1936, an Argyllshire party worker confessed to worries that the seat might be regained by the Liberals, although it had been Tory for some twelve years.[84]

It was perhaps in the agricultural areas that the Unionists felt the greatest pressure from the Liberals. Although the Unionists had made great inroads into these seats in the 1920s, traditionally the Scottish farming vote – as distinct from the English experience – had been predominantly Liberal. There remained the worry for Tories that if circumstances altered, the Liberals might revive there. In the 1930s the crisis in Scottish agriculture fanned worries about the fragility of the farmers' new-found commitment to Unionism. The depression in farming persisted in Scotland for most of the decade, and the government's handling of the problem was doubly, if slightly contradictorily, criticised. It was blamed for failing to act to relieve the hardship: there were hostile resolutions at several party conferences right up until 1938.[85] Then, its strenuous efforts to rectify the causes of the difficulty only intensified the farmers' wrath.

The Milk Marketing Board, established in 1933, was a particular target.[86] The different treatment meted out to English and Scottish grain growers was another focus for grievance: a subsidy was given to wheat, but not to barley and oats, these last two being of course the Scottish arable staples.[87] When, on the eve of war, the subsidy was at last extended to oats, Boothby leant over to the MP for Kincardine & West Aberdeenshire and said:'Kemsley, this has made your seat safe for life.'[88]

Accordingly, great concern was shown not to alienate Liberals. In the critical Carlton Club meeting of 1922 the overwhelming majority of Scottish Tory MPs voted to keep the Coalition in being, while English Tories heavily backed its dissolution.[89] In 1925 Kilmarnock Unionists refused to distribute the party news-sheet because they felt that its contents would offend Liberals.[90] In the 1930s, this edginess persisted. A senior figure stressed that,'he could not but think that there was a large body of opinion in the country which might regard itself as Liberal-National or National Labour', and he pointed out that many of the fifty Unionist MPs owed their seats to such individuals.[91]

One significant upshot was that the Unionists in Scotland were far more disposed to reach election deals with Liberals and were more concerned at any potential damage to these liaisons than was the case in England. In the 1922 contest, the Scots were left free by Central Office to strike deals with Liberals, whereas in England there was less co-operation. This informal deal-brokering was in operation in subsequent elections, although the degree of harmony varied.[92] The 1931 election reinforces the impression of Scottish distinctiveness in two ways. Firstly, whereas in England there were a number of seats where there was a three-way fight between Labour, Liberal and Tory, in Scotland there was only one. Where Liberal and Tory entered the same field, it was because there was no Labour presence. The second feature of this election followed on: in Scotland, proportionately more Liberal and National Liberal MPs were returned than in England. In 1935, too, although the virtually watertight arrangements of 1931 were fraying, there was in general still pretty good co-ordination between the two parties.

The importance of conciliating Liberals was highlighted by the Greenock by-election of 1936, caused by the death of the sitting Liberal, Sir Godfrey Collins. The Unionists rejected the two Liberal nominations for the contest (a local baillie and a former National Liberal MP), instead pressing on the constituency one of their own.

Although he ran as an unadorned 'National', Liberal voter's were enraged at what they regarded as their reserved right to nominate being breached. While the local Liberal paper tried to patch matters up, there was a high quota of disaffection which resulted in Labour capturing the seat. Yet in the municipal election held earlier in the same month, the anti-Labour forces had won three seats from Labour, so regaining control of the town council.[93]

One aspect of this bid to woo Liberals was to argue that Liberalism was an anachronistic, essentially nineteenth century movement, but now 'the Unionists were carrying forward the underlying values of the former.'[94] The Tories therefore, as is explained by Elaine McFarland elsewhere in this volume, became increasingly distant from the device of playing the Orange working-class card, which had been dabbled with in pre-war years. The party, of course, would not spurn such support, but as a general rule, it did not strive officiously to solicit it. In the later 1930s, it is interesting to note, the Scottish Unionist Association carefully detached itself from involvement with a renewed Ulster loyalist agitation.[95]

The Tories also took a firm stand against right-wing extremism. The eruption of political protestant militancy in both Glasgow and Edinburgh which began in 1932 was studiously rebuffed by the party. Sectarianism, it roundly declared, had no place in British politics. It was the Unionists and their local government fronts, the Moderates and Progressives, who were electorally the main casualties of the impact of Cormack and Ratcliffe. The response in Glasgow was to reconstruct the Progressive party as a more effective fighting force, but close links with Liberals were actively promoted in the revived organisation.[96]

Similarly, the Tories were resolutely opposed to any linkages with fascism. Only the paranoid Duchess of Atholl, firmly persuaded that the hills of Perthshire were alive to the sound not of music but of Fascists baying for her blood, seemed to doubt this. When the right-wing Col. Thomas Moore wrote an article 'The Blackshirts Have What the Tories Need', he was severely reprimanded by party officials. The Fascists and the Communists were linked in a robust denunciation of their 'revolutionary and anti-democratic policies', while Baldwin's government was applauded for its resistance to 'subversive forces'.[97]

In the 1930s the Tories were much exercised by the challenge which the rise of Scottish nationalism was seen to pose. Drawing support from Liberals and Tories, the Scottish Party (est. 1932), unlike the more radical, socialistic National Party of Scotland, sharpened this perception.[98] One grass-roots activist noted with apprehension, the lure the Scottish National Party (after 1933) presented to moderate Liberals and Unionists alike.[99] The extent to which such thinking had permeated the party was most evident in Cathcart. Here, the Unionist association secretary, Kevin Macdowall, was expelled in 1932 because of his pro-nationalist views. Almost all the office-bearers and a high proportion of the activists left with him. This episode encouraged a state of concern in the party and in 1932 the Western District Council set up a committee to investigate the challenge of Scottish Home Rule. A leaflet was produced later that year, outlining the menace presented by the nationalist movement.[100]

The response of the Tories was firstly to reiterate their total commitment to the union, stressing in particular the economic benefits it had yielded. But in addition, as is shown by James Mitchell elsewhere in this volume, concessions to Home Rule opinion were made: the Gilmour Report presaged an extension of administrative devolution to the Scottish Office. It was often stressed that it was a Conservative administration which had accomplished the elevation of the Scottish Secretary to the loftier eminence of a Secretary of State and the building of St Andrew's House, completed in 1939, was the physical symbol of the Conservatives' support for self-government.[101] The need to appease Scottish sensitivities was used by the Scottish Office in the 1930s to try to secure preferential treatment for Scotland in a number of social and economic matters.[102]

One method by which Liberal susceptibilities were soothed and a progressive image in dealing with Scottish affairs conveyed is revealed by analysis of the holders of the post of Scottish Secretary in Unionist and Unionist-dominated administrations. There were four Liberals, but only three Unionists.[103] The Unionists who held the office were all drawn from the liberal wing of the party, and indeed the last one (Colville) had stood as a Lloyd George Liberal candidate in 1922.

Another means of keeping Liberals on board was to have MPs who were seen as representing the non-reactionary wing of Unionism. This trend became more marked as the inter-war years advanced. By the 1930s there were few die-hards, apart from MacQuisten, Moore and Ramsay. On the other hand, progressive

Tories seemed to abound, and the prominence of Elliot, Buchan and Skelton underlined the influence of the moderate tendency. Elliot, after all, had begun his political involvement as a socialist, and always retained a centrist approach. He did not believe in the market being left unfettered and systematically championed the concept of interventionist central state activity. It was during his term at the Department of Agriculture that the first firm steps towards a corporatist policy were taken.[104]

Others pursuing left-leaning tendencies included Robert Boothby, who, in the 1930s, aligned himself with Tory radical dissidents like MacMillan, advocating a forward policy on social and economic planning. Boothby defined his position in the inter-war years thus: 'I am a progressive MP for a progressive constituency.'[105] The Duchess of Atholl, particularly through her championing of the republican side in the Spanish Civil War and later opposition to appeasement, also established an image to which Liberals might respond.[106] Many of these Tories seemed, to the naked eye, indistinguishable from Liberals. The Duke and Duchess of Atholl had, in the early 1920s, advocated the creation of a centre party, forged from Liberals and reforming Tories. Liberals did not run against Boothby in his Aberdeenshire seat because they regarded him as one of them.

So, while recent work has tended to cast doubt on the depth of liberal Tory beliefs in England, there was certainly no lack of commitment in Scotland.[107] Here the adoption of interventionist, socially engaged policies was a central theme. This reassured Liberals that the Unionists were not die-hards, and it also enabled Tories to reach out to working-class voters. An emphasis on social reform, it was contended by a constituency women's organiser, would be of special interest to women: 'Why should they leave the Labour Party to bring forward all the great social evils? They [women] wanted to get into the Unionist party – progressive and kindly people who were really out for the good of the country.'[108] Fully a decade later, the message was reiterated in the claim that Unionism 'has no lack of sympathy for the "underdog". One of its main objects throughout its history has been to raise the standard of life of the people. it has done much to improve it and it will continue to do so.'[109]

On a broad range of social policy matters, a relatively advanced stance was adopted by the Unionists. In addition to a key focus on housing, there were repeated calls for better pension schemes. The grounds for this included: 'realising that on our production and successful operation of such a scheme depends to an incalculable extent the permanent betterment of social conditions.'[110] The pension measure of 1925 was acclaimed as 'probably the most humane and beneficial measure of social reform seen in this generation', and this was echoed in the extolling of the British social services a decade later as 'unrivalled' and the most generous in the world.[111] Unemployment was repeatedly deplored as a 'clamant evil' and a 'source of much concern' to the party. While there was confidence that economic recovery would eventually eliminate the problem, in the interim the improvement in benefit levels for the workless introduced by Unionists was highlighted.[112] Walter Elliot's pioneering of free school milk schemes, begun on an experimental basis in the seven larger cities in 1927, and extended throughout the country in a bill of 1929, was an important instance of this liberal Toryism.[113]

Unfettered capitalism was regarded as antiquated in the contemporary economic climate and inimical to social well-being. The former was stressed by the voice of the Clydeside business class, the *Glasgow Herald*, urging rejection of siren calls for free trade. The latter was underscored by an official party pamphlet of 1935 which announced the Unionist 'belief in the authority of the state over private interests for the good of the whole community', which resulted in a desire to develop simultaneously 'the instruments of comradeship and social service and the instruments of independence and industry'.[114] Public expenditure to create jobs and develop the infrastructure was treated as quite acceptable: a Forth-Clyde canal was mooted on these grounds, with the example of a similar project at Marseilles cited as proof of its value.[115] The party was not as virulently hostile to trade unions as some wished: the Western Council voted by three to one against supporting a bill to end the political levy system, while a resolution calling for extreme measures to curb union rights was rejected in favour of a more moderate reform.[116]

The Tories also took a lively interest in the problems of the Highlands, calling for the transport and medical care infrastructure to be improved. Moreover, this was to be borne not by local government finances, but by central government. In the general context noted above, of an assumption of minimal public spending levels and an impulse against increasing tax levels, this was a very unusual position to adopt.[117]

Again, the Tories seemed able to contemplate electoral reform with equanimity in this period, as distinct from their generally hostile attitude before 1914. The extension of the vote to all women in 1928 was generally warmly applauded. The chair of the Central

Council contended that the influx of first-time voters should not be held responsible for the party's set-back in the 1929 general election.[118] The party even took up the case for reform of the House of Lords, an old Liberal cry. At the 1925 and 1926 Annual Conferences of the Scottish Unionist Association, resolutions were carried advocating altering the composition of the upper chamber. This was, to some extent, less radical than it appeared: a second house with a stronger democratic mandate could more legitimately use its delaying powers to block any future Labour government's legislation.[119]

The extent of the change in inter-war Unionism, in comparison to its pre-1914 image, was remarked on enthusiastically by a prominent ILP member of parliament in 1926. He praised the Scottish Secretary for doing 'such splendid things': 'Your actions so little resemble the Toryism of my youth.' The result was to blur the partisan divide: 'I believe the rigidity of party lines is slackening'.[120] This judgment may be verified on a wider sampling basis. Whereas in the 1945 general election the swing in England was 12.1 per cent away from the Tories, in Scotland it was substantially lower, at 8.6 per cent. This election is frequently regarded as, in good part, a verdict on the party's inter-war performance. This would suggest that in the eyes of the voters there were fewer guilty men (and women) in Scottish Unionism.

NOTES

1. A. Seldon & S. Ball, *Conservative Century: The Conservative Party since 1900* (Oxford, 1994), pp. 59, 326.
2. Duchess of Atholl, *Women and Politics* (London, 1931), Chs. 8–13.
3. W. Elliot, *Toryism in the Twentieth Century* (London, 1927).
4. Cf. C. Coote, *A Companion of Honour. The Story of Walter Elliot in Scotland and Westminster* (London, 1965), pp. 99–101.
5. E. E. M. Taylor, *The Politics of Walter Elliot, 1929–36* (Edinburgh University Ph.D. thesis, 1979), pp. 72–4.
6. National Library of Scotland, Scottish Conservative and Unionist Association MSS, Acc. 10424/27(iv), Scottish Unionist Association, *Annual Report*, 1924–5; Scottish Unionist Association Eastern Divisional Council, *Ann. Reps.*, 1923–4, 1924–5.
7. NLS, SCUA MSS, Acc. 10424/27(v), Scottish Unionist Association W[estern] D[ivisional] C[ouncil], *Ann. Rep.*, 1928–9.
8. *Ibid.*, Acc. 10424/27(v, vii), Scottish Unionist Association WDC, *Ann. Reps.*, 1928–9, cf. 1934–5, 1936–7; also EDC, *Ann. Rep.*, 1936–7.

9. *Ibid.*, Acc. 10424/27(iv), Scottish Unionist Association EDC, WDC *Ann. Reps.*, 1926–7.
10. *Ibid.*, Acc 10424/27(vii), Scottish Unionist Association, *Ann. Rep.*, 1936–7. Cf Acc. 10424/27(vi,vii), Scottish Unionist Association WDC, *Ann. Rep.*, 1932-3; Scottish Unionist Association, *Ann. Rep.*, 1934–5, 1935–6; Acc. 10424/26(vii), G[lasgow] U[nionist] A[ssociation], *Ann. Rep.*, 1933 (Tradeston CA), 1937; Acc. 10424/32, WDC Minute Book, 12 Jan. 1938.
11. *Stirling Journal*, 3 Mar. 1938.
12. *Stirling Journal*, 2 Nov. 1939.
13. NLS, SCUA MSS, Acc. 10424/27(viii), Scottish Unionist Association WDC, *Ann. Rep.*, 1938–9.
14. *Ibid.*, Acc. 10424/29, Scottish Unionist Association, WDC Min. Bk., 1 Apr. 1925, 3 Mar. 1926, 4 May 1927; Acc. 10424/27(v), WDC, *Ann. Rep.*, 1929–30.
15. *Ibid.*, Acc. 10424/27(vi), Scottish Unionist Association WDC, *Ann. Rep.*, 1934–5.
16. *Ibid.*, Acc. 10424/27(vi), Scottish Unionist Association EDC, *Ann. Rep.*, 1931–2.
17. *Ibid.*, Acc. 10424/27(vii), Scottish Unionist Association WDC, *Ann. Rep.*, 1938-9.
18. *Ibid.*, Acc. 10424/26(vii), GUA, *Ann. Rep.*, 1937 (St Rollox CA).
19. *Ibid.*, Acc. 10424/26(vi), GUA, *Ann. Rep.*, 1936, (Kelvingrove CA).
20. *Ibid.*, Acc. 10424/26(vii,viii), GUA, *Ann. Reps.* 1937, 1938 (Maryhill, St Rollox CA).
21. *Ibid.*, Acc. 10424/27(vii), Scottish Unionist Association, *Ann. Rep.*, 1935–6, WDC, *Ann. Rep.*, 1936–87.
22. *Ibid.*, Acc. 10424/64, Scottish Unionist Association, Central Council Min. Bk., 13 Dec. 1929; Acc. 10424/27(vi), Scottish Unionist Association EDC, *Ann. Rep.*, 1934–5.
23. I.e., Unionist: Duchess of Atholl (West Perth & Kinross), 1923–38; F. Horsburgh (Dundee), 1935–45; H. Shaw (Bothwell), 1931–35. Labour: J. Lee (Lanarkshire, Northern), 1929–31; A. Hardie (Rutherglen), 1931–1945.
24. NLS, SCUA MSS, Acc 10424/27(iv), Scottish Unionist Association EDC, *Ann. Rep.*, 1923–4.
25. *Ibid.*, Acc. 10424/27 Scottish Unionist Association EDC, WDC *Ann. Reps.*, 1925–6.
26. *Ibid.*, Acc. 10424/27, Scottish Unionist Association EDC, WDC *Ann. Reps.*, 1926–7.
27. *Ibid.*, Acc. 10424/31, Scottish Unionist Association WDC Min. Bk., 13 Jan. 1932; Acc. 10424/27(vii), Scottish Unionist Association EDC, *Ann. Rep.*, 1937–8. Cf. Acc. 10424/29, Scottish Unionist Association WDC Min. Bk., 17 Dec. 1924; Acc. 10424/27(iv,v), Scottish Unionist Association EDC, *Ann. Rep.*, 1926–7, 1927–8; Acc. 10424/27(vi,vii), Scottish Unionist Association WDC, Ann. Reps., 1931–2, 1935–6.
28. *Ibid.*, Acc. 10424/29, Scottish Unionist Association WDC Min. Bk., 1 Dec. 1926, 8 Jan. 1927, 7 Apr. 1926.
29. *Ibid.*, Acc. 10424/279, Scottish Unionist Association EDC, *Ann. Rep.*, 1935–6.
30. *Ibid.*, Acc. 10424/27(iv), Scottish Unionist Association WDC, *Ann. Rep.*, 1923–4.

31. *Ibid.*, Acc. 10424/27(v), Scottish Unionist Association EDC, *Ann. Reps.*, 1927–8, 1928–9; WDC, *Ann. Rep.*, 1929–30.
32. *Ibid.*, Acc. 10424/27(iv), Scottish Unionist Association WDC, *Ann. Rep.*, 1923–4.
33. *Ibid.*, Acc. 10424/27(iv), Scottish Unionist Association WDC, *Ann. Rep.*, 1923–4; Acc. 10424/29 Scottish Unionist Association WDC Min. Bk., 4 June 1924.
34. *Ibid.*, Acc.10424/27(iv), Scottish Unionist Association, *Ann. Rep.*, 1923–4.
35. *Ibid.*, Acc. 10424/27(vi,vii), Scottish Unionist Association WDC, *Ann. Rep.*, 1934–5, 1935–6.
36. *Ibid.*, Acc. 10424/27(v), Scottish Unionist Association EDC, *Ann. Rep.*, 1928–9; WDC, *Ann. Reps.*, 1929–30, 1930–1.
37. *Ibid.*, Acc. 10424/27(vii), Scottish Unionist Association, *Ann. Rep.*, 1935–6.
38. *Ibid.*, Acc. 10424/27(v), Scottish Unionist Association WDC, *Ann. Rep.*, 1930-1; Acc 10424/31, Scottish Unionist Association WDC Min. Bk., 6 Apr. 1932.
39. *Ibid.*, Acc. 10424/27(v), Scottish Unionist Association WDC, *Ann. Reps.*, 1923–4, 1926–7.
40. *Ibid.*, Acc. 10424/27(vi, vii), Scottish Unionist Association EDC, *Ann. Rep.*, 1934-5; WDC, *Ann. Reps.*, 1934–5, 1935–6.
41. *Ibid.*, Acc. 10424/64, Scottish Unionist Association Central Council Min. Bk., 25 Feb. 1928, 1 Feb. 1938.
42. *Ibid.*, Acc. 10424/27(vii), Scottish Unionist Association WDC, *Ann. Rep.*, 1936–7, 1937–8 (for a case in Stirling).
43. *Ibid.*, Acc. 10424/27(vii), Scottish Unionist Association WDC, *Ann. Rep.*, 1935–6.
44. *Ibid.*, Acc. 10424/27(iv), Scottish Unionist Association WDC, *Ann. Reps.*, 1923–4.
45. *Ibid.*, Acc. 10424/26(vii), GUA, *Ann. Rep.*, 1935 (Bridgeton, Partick and Pollok C.A.s).
46. *Ibid.*, Acc. 10424/27(vi), Scottish Unionist Association WDC, *Ann. Reps.*, 1931–2, 1934–5; Acc 10424/31, Scottish Unionist Association WDC Min. Bk., 31 May 1933.
47. *Ibid.*, Acc. 10424/27(vi, vii), Scottish Unionist Association WDC, *Ann. Reps.*, 1934–5, 1935–6; Acc. 10424/26(vi), GUA, *Ann. Rep.*, 1933 (Kelvingrove C.A.)
48. *Ibid.*, Acc. 10424/27(iv-vii), Scottish Unionist Association EDC, *Ann. Reps.*, 1926–7, 1927–8, 1933–4; Scottish Unionist Association, *Ann. Rep.*, 1935–6; Scottish Unionist Association WDC, *Ann. Rep.*, 1937–8.
49. *Ibid.*, Acc. 10424/64, Scottish Unionist Association Central Committee Min. Bk., 8 Nov. 19367: Acc. 10424/32, Scottish Unionist Association WDC, Min. Bk., 10 Mar. 1937.
50. *Ibid.*, Acc. 10424/64, Scottish Unionist Association Central Council Min. Bk., 21 Feb. 1934.
51. *Ibid.*, Acc. 10424/63, Scottish Unionist Association Central Council Min. Bk., 14 July 1926.
52. *Ibid.*, Acc. 10424/64, Scottish Unionist Association Central Council Min. Bk., 7 July, 9 Dec. 1936.

53. *Ibid.*, Acc. 10424/26(v), GUA, *Ann. Reps.*, 1927, (Cathcart CA); cf. J.H. Young, *A History of Cathcart Conservative and Unionist Association: 1918 to 1993* (n.p., n.d.), Appendix.
54. NLS, SCUA MSS, Acc. 100424/27(iv), Scottish Unionist Association EDC, *Ann. Rep.*, 1923–4.
55. Derived from *ibid.*, Acc. 10424/27(iv–vii), Scottish Unionist Association, *Ann. Reps.*, 1919–20 –1938–9.
56. *Ibid.*, Acc. 10424/27(vi), Scottish Unionist Association, EDC, WDC *Ann. Reps.*, 1931–2.
57. *Ibid.*, Acc. 10424/32, Scottish Unionist Association WDC Min. Bk., 5 Apr. 1939.
58. *Ibid.*, Acc. 10424/27(vi), Scottish Unionist Association EDC, *Ann. Rep.*, 1931–2.
59. Young, *Cathcart Conservative Association*, p. 35.
60. NLS, SCUA MSS Acc. 10424/26(vii), GUA, *Ann. Rep.*, 1934, (Cathcart CA).
61. I. G. C. Hutchison, *A Political History of Scotland, 1832–1924* (Edinburgh, 1986) p. 316.
62. The former had actually begun in 1914 as the Post, but its take-off in popularity really only dates from the end of the war.
63. Hutchison, *A Political History*, p. 224.
64. See S. J. Brown: '"A Solemn Purification by Fire": Responses to the Great War in the Scottish Presbyterian Churches', *Journal of Ecclesiastical History*, 45 (1994), pp. 82-104; '"A Victory for God": Scottish Presbyterian Churches and the General Strike of 1926', *Ibid.*, 42 (1991), pp. 596–617.
65. A. Muir, *John White* (London, 1958). White was a member of the Scottish Conservative Club, an elite Tory institution.
66. In addition, a remarkable 25 Liberals and 8 Unionists were barristers.
67. NLS, SCUA MSS, Acc. 10424/7(vi), Shedden MSS, P. Blair to L. Shedden, 27, 28 Apr. 1937.
68. I. G. C. Hutchison, 'The Scottish Nobility and Politics, c.1880–1939', in T. M. Devine (ed.), *Scottish Elites* (Edinburgh, 1994), pp. 144–5.
69. R. J. Finlay, '"For or Against?" Scottish Nationalists and the British Empire, 1919-39', *Scottish Historical Review*, 71 (1992), pp. 184–206.
70. Hutchison, *A Political History*; p. 242–5; L. Leneman, *Fit for Heroes? Land Settlement in Scotland after the First World War* (Aberdeen, 1989); E.A. Cameron, *Land for the People? The British Government and the Scottish Highlands, c.1880–1925* (East Linton, 1996); Hutchison, 'The Scottish Nobility and Politics', pp. 137–8, 142–3.
71. Hutchison, *A Political History*, pp. 322, 327.
72. *Glasgow Herald*, 13 Nov. 1935.
73. *Alloa Advertiser*, 24 Oct. 1931; cf. NLS, SCUA MSS, Acc. 10424/31, Scottish Unionist Association WDC Min. Bk., 7 Dec. 1932 for another instance.
74. S[cottish] R[ecords] O[ffice], Steel-Maitland MSS, GD 193/24/16, J, Monteath to Lady Steel-Maitland, 23 Aug., 27 Sept., 6 Oct. 1918; cf. *Stirling Journal*, 14 Nov. 1918. More generally, see G. Brown, 'The Labour Party and Political Change in Scotland, 1918–29: The Politics of Five Elections', (Edinburgh University, Ph.D. Thesis, 1982), pp. 79–88.

75. NLS, SCUA MSS, Acc. 10424/27(iv), Scottish Unionist Association, *Ann. Rep.*, 1924-5; Hutchison, *A Political History*, pp. 326–8; Brown, *Labour Party and Political Change*, pp. 326–61.
76. NLS, SCUA, MSS, Acc. 104524/126.
77. *Alloa Advertiser*, 17 Oct. 1931, cf. 24 Oct. 1931.
78. Brown, *Labour Party and Political Change*, pp. 289–96; Hutchison, *A Political History*, p. 322.
79. Glasgow, McRoberts Solicitors, W. Renfrewshire Conservative Association MSS, W. Perry to S. Baldwin, 30 October 1923.
80. NLS, SCUA MSS, Acc. 10424/30, Scottish Unionist Association, WDC Min. Bk., 5 June 1929.
81. Cf. Hutchison, *A Political History*, p. 284.
82. *Alloa Advertiser*, 13 Apr. 1929.
83. NLS, SCUA MSS, Acc. 10424/30, Scottish Unionist Association WDC Min. Bk., 5 June 1929.
84. NLS, SCUA MSS, Acc. 10424/32, Scottish Unionist Association WDC Min. Bk., 4 Mar. 1936.
85. *Ibid.*, Acc. 100424/31, Scottish Unionist Association WDC Min. Bk., 13 Jan. 1932; Acc. 10424/64, Scottish Unionist Association Central Council Min. Bk., 17 Nov. 1938.
86. *Ibid.*, Acc. 10424/27(vi, vii), Scottish Unionist Association, *Ann. Reps.*, 1933–4, 1936–7, 1937–8; Acc. 10424/64, Scottish Unionist Association Central Council Min. Bk., 23 Nov. 1934, 29 Nov. 1935; Acc. 10424/31, Scottish Unionist Association WDC Min. Bk., 30 May 1934, 29 May 1935.
87. *Ibid.*, Acc. 10424/64, Scottish Unionist Association Central Council Min. Bk., 17 Nov., 16 May 1933.
88. C. Thornton-Kemsley, *Through Winds and Tides* (Montrose, 1974), p. 107.
89. Hutchison, *A Political History*, p. 314 for the details.
90. NLS, SCUA MSS, Acc. 10424/29, Scottish Unionist Association WDC Min. Bk., 4 Mar. 1925.
91. *Ibid.*, Acc. 10424/64, Scottish Unionist Association Central Council Min. Bk., 21 Feb. 1934.
92. Brown, 'Labour Party and Political Change', Chs. 4, 5, 6, 9.
93. NLS, Scottish Secretariat MSS, Acc. 3721/68/329, various press-cuttings, 23 Oct. to 26 Nov. 1936.
94. *Questions of the Day*, pp. 7–10; cf. p. 31.
95. NLS, SCUA MSS, Acc. 10424/64, Scottish Unionist Association Central Council Min. Bk., 1 Feb. 1938.
96. *Ibid.*, Acc. 10424/31-2, Scottish Unionist Association WDC Min. Bk., 6 Dec. 1933, [7 Feb. 1934], 4 Mar. 1936, 3 Nov. 1937. For the general context, see T. Gallagher, 'Protestant Extremism in Urban Scotland, 1930–9: Its Growth and Contraction', *Scottish Historical Review*, 64 (1985), pp. 143–67.
97. NLS, SCUA MSS, Acc. 10424/26(vii), GUA, *Ann. Rep.*, 1937; Acc. 10424/64, Scottish Unionist Association Central Council Min. Bk., 18 Nov. 1936.
98. R. J. Finlay, *Independent or Free? Scottish Politics and the Origins of the Scottish National Party, 1918–45* (Edinburgh, 1994), pp. 71–205.
99. NLS, SCUA MSS, Acc. 10424/31, Scottish Unionist Association WDC Min. Bk., 7 Nov. 1934.

100. *Ibid.*, Acc. 10424/31, Scottish Unionist Association WDC Min. Bk., 6 Apr., 4 May, 7 Sept., 5 Oct. 1932, 11 Jan., 1 Mar. 1933, 7 Nov. 1934.

101. J. Mitchell, *Conservatives and the Union: A Study of Conservative Party Attitudes to Scotland* (Edinburgh, 1990), pp. 21–6, 45–8; Mitchell, 'The Gilmour Report on Scottish Central Administration', *Juridical Review*, (1989), pp. 173–88. See also, L. Paterson, *The Autonomy of Modern Scotland* (Edinburgh, 1994), pp. 104–11.

102. R. H. Campbell,'The Scottish Office and the Special Areas in the 1930s', *Historical Journal*, 22 (1979), pp. 167–84; I. G. C. Hutchison,'The Scottish Office and the Scottish Universities, c.1930 – c.1960', in J. J. Carter & D. J. Withrington, *Scottish Universities. Distinctiveness and Diversity* (Edinburgh, 1992), pp. 56–66.

103. Liberals: R. Munro (1918–22), Lord Novar (1922–3), A. Sinclair (1931–2), Sir G. Collins, 1932–6; Unionists: J. Gilmour (1924–9), W. Elliot (1936–8), J. Colville (1938–40). Colville was briefly succeeded in 1940–1 by another National Liberal, A. E. Brown.

104. Coote, *Companion of Honour*, pp. 108–9, 132–46; Taylor, *Politics of W. Elliot*, pp. 193–400.

105. R. R. James, *Bob Boothby: A Portrait* (London, 1991), p. 67, cf. 154–5; for his social policy views, see pp. 67, 72–4, 133, 155–7, 185–9, 234–5.

106. S. J. Hetherington, *Katharine Atholl, 1874–1960. Against the Tide* (Aberdeen, 1989); S. Ball, 'The Politics of Appeasement: the Fall of the Duchess of Atholl and the Kinross and West Perth By-election, December 1938', *Scottish Historical Review*, 69 (1990), pp. 49–83.

107. E.g., M. Bentley,'Liberal Toryism in the Twentieth Century', *Transactions of the Royal Historical Society*, Sixth Series, 4 (1994), pp. 177–202; J. Ramsden, "A Party for Owners or a Party for Earners? How far did the British Conservative Party Really Change after 1945?', *ibid.*, Fifth Series, 37 (1987), pp. 49–63; J. Barnes,'Ideology and Factions', in Seldon & Ball, *Conservative Century*, pp. 315–45.

108. *Stirling Journal*, 15 Mar. 1923.

109. NLS, SCUA MSS, Acc. 10424/27(vi), Scottish Unionist Association, *Ann. Rep.*, 1934–5.

110. *Ibid.*, Acc. 10424/29,Scottish Unionist Association WDC Min. Bk., 10 Nov. 1924; Acc. 10424/63, Central Council Min. Bk., 3 Nov. 1927, 22 Nov. 1928; Acc. 10424/27(v,vi), Scottish Unionist Association EDC, *Ann. Rep.*, 1928–9, Scottish Unionist Association, *Ann. Rep.*, 1932-3. Cf. *Questions of the Day*, pp. 22–3, 37–44.

111. *Ibid.*, Acc. 10424/(27(iv,vi), Scottish Unionist Association, *Ann. Rep.*, 1924–5, 1933–4; cf. *The National Government. What Has It Done? What Is It Doing?* (Edinburgh, 1935), pp. 10–11.

112. NLS, SCUA MSS, Acc. 10424/63,64, Scottish Unionist Association Central Council Min. Bk., 13 Nov. 1925, (cf. 30. Nov. 1933); Acc. 10424/26(vi), GUA, *Ann. Rep.*, 1933; Acc. 10424/27(vi), Scottish Unionist Association, *Ann. Rep.*, 1933–4; *National Government*, pp. 3–4.

113. Coote, *Companion of Honour*, pp. 112–6; for other examples of Elliot's social conscience, see pp. 69–74, 82–9, 106–8, 186–92. Cf. Taylor, Politics of W. Elliot, pp. 39–45, 69–70, 103–5.

114. *The National Government*, pp. 17–18.

115. NLS, SCUA MSS, Acc. 10424/31, Scottish Unionist Association WDC Min. Bk., 3 May 1933.
116. *Ibid.*, Acc. 10424/29, Scottish Unionist Association WDC Min. Bk 4 March 1925.; Acc. 10424/63, Central Council Min. Bk., 13 Nov. 1925.
117. *Ibid.*, Acc. 10424/64, Scottish Unionist Association Central Council Min. Bk., 13 Dec. 1929, 23 Nov. 1934: Acc. 10424/32, WDC Min. Bk., 4 Mar. 1936.
118. *Ibid.*, Acc. 10424/63, Scottish Unionist Association Central Council Min. Bk., 12 Nov. 1926, 3 Nov. 1927, 11 September 1929.
119. *Ibid.*, Acc. 10424/63, Scottish Unionist Association, Central Council Min. Bk., 13 Nov.1925, 12 Nov. 1926.
120. Scottish Records Office, Gilmour of Montrave MSS, GD 393/23/6, E.R. Mitchell to J. Gilmour, 15 February 1926.

APPENDIX

Table 5.1 The Conservative Share of the Vote, 1922–35 (%)

Election	England	Scotland	Wales
1922	41.5	25.1	21.4
1923	39.8	31.6	21.1
1924	47.7	40.7	28.4
1929	38.8	35.9	22.0
1931	57.8	49.5	22.1
1935	49.4	42.0	23.4

NOTE: *The 1918 election is disregarded, because of the exceptional circumstances in which it was fought.*
SOURCE: F. W. S. Craig, *British Parliamentary Facts, 1932–1987* (Fifth Edition, Aldershot, 1989), Tables 1.22–1.27.

Table 5.2 The Ratio of the Conservative Vote between England, Scotland and Wales, 1922 and 1935

	England	Scotland	Wales
1922	100	60.5	51.6
1935	100	85.0	47.4

SOURCE: Craig, *British Parliamentary Facts*, Tables 1.22–1.27

Table 5.3 The Politics of the Scottish Press, 1913–38

	1913	*1938*
Unionist	51	31
Liberal	59	13
Independent	55	58
Neutral	20	14
Not Given	26	61

NOTE: *These figures cover all Scottish newspapers, including the four large cities*
SOURCE: *Newspaper Press Directory*, (London, 1913; 1938)

Table 5.4 Liberal Voters and MPs, 1922–35

	England *% Vote*	*% MPs*	*Scotland* *% Vote*	*% MPs*
1922	19.6	9.1	21.5	21.1
1923	29.9	27.4	28.4	31.0
1924	17.6	3.9	16.6	11.3
1929	23.6	7.2	18.1	18.3
1931	5.8	3.9	8.6	9.9
1935	6.3	2.3	6.7	4.2

SOURCE: Craig, *British Parliamentary Facts*, Tables 1.22–1.27

6

UNIONISM AND THE DEPENDENCY CULTURE: POLITICS AND STATE INTERVENTION IN SCOTLAND, 1918–1997

Richard J. Finlay

The Children of Adam

One of the key features, if not *the* key feature, of Scottish politics in the 1980s was the decline of the Conservative Party. That the land of Adam Smith should reject the free market ideology of the Conservative governments of the eighties caused Mrs Thatcher considerable consternation. Indeed, in her memoirs she made pointed reference to the fact that the Scottish Office secured higher rates of public expenditure north of the border which, far from being a cause of shame, was a source of great pride.[1] Thatcher's failure to comprehend the reasons why the Scots showed a greater political proclivity towards state intervention coincided with some of the cruder 'jock baiting' of her junior colleagues who talked about a dependency culture in Scotland. They coined the phrase 'subsidy junkie', which was used as a term of abuse for a society which had rejected the individualist values which had spearheaded the Thatcher revolution south of the border. Yet few were aware of the role that their own great party had in promoting this state of affairs. Indeed, it was a sin of which all British parties were guilty, because state intervention and economic links to the south were the central components in the political evolution of unionist ideology in the period after the First World War.[2]

Before going any further, it is necessary to elucidate what is meant by unionism. Although the concept has been hijacked in recent years for exclusive use by the Conservative Party to define support for the constitutional *status quo*, the meaning of the word has historically been much broader (see the chapter by James Mitchell in this volume). For the purposes of this essay, it is necessary to define what might be called small'u'unionism as opposed to capital'U'unionism. The former might be broadly defined as the belief that Scotland should remain part of the British state apparatus. In this sense, all the British political parties are unionist because, although some of them at various times have toyed with the idea of setting up a Scottish parliament, at no time have they advocated dismantling the British state. The latter Unionism is associated with the Conservative Party, and although born from a desire to maintain the Union with Ireland in the late nineteenth century, in the period after the First World War it has become increasingly identified with that particular party's hostility to demands for Scottish home rule.[3]

It is the objective of this essay to chart the ways in which economic dependency on England and the British state apparatus have moulded unionist ideology in the twentieth century. Indeed, it will be argued that this has been its most important strand. The period has been divided into three key sections which seek to tackle the issue chronologically. The first will examine how unionism became increasingly dependent on economic arguments in the inter-war period as an antidote to the political consequences of the structural dislocation which affected the Scottish economy and the rise of nationalist sentiment. The second section will analyse how state planning was central to the political ideology of all the British parties in Scotland after the Second World War as a means to achieve economic and social regeneration. Finally, the problems and contradictions which have been experienced by unionism in the era after 1979 when attempts were made to reduce state activity in the economy and society will be explored.

1918–1939: Relying on the 'Richer Country'

Unionism in the period from 1886 to 1914 was characterised by confidence in Scotland's contribution to the imperial partnership. The Union was portrayed as a dynamic combination of Scottish and English prowess and the Scots took great pride in the way that their nation contributed to British imperial, military and economic achievement. The Scots, it was argued, had provided the British state and empire with some of its best soldiers, missionaries, explorers, scientists, engineers, businessmen, prime ministers and administrators.[4] Glasgow rejoiced in its self-proclaimed title that it was the 'Second City of the Empire' and for many politicians such as Lord

Rosebery, it was a cardinal statement of fact that the Scots were over-achievers in the Union and the British imperial mission.[5] While many historians have often focused their scholarly attention on the divisions within Scottish society in this period, it is worth pointing out that the sanctity of the Union was one of the few issues which commanded a near universal consensus in Scottish intellectual and political circles. Indeed, even when examining the home rule campaign of the Edwardian era, one finds that one of the principal reasons for promoting the creation of a Scottish parliament was that it would lead to greater imperial efficiency and up-date and modernise the Union. Far from presenting a challenge to the Union, Scottish home rule was promoted in the belief that it would strengthen and revitalise the partnership between Scotland and England.[6] Yet the impact of the First World War and its aftermath was to test such assumptions as Scottish society experienced fundamental political, economic and social dislocation.[7]

Although support in Labour circles for Scottish home rule after the First World War carried on into the mid 1920s, it soon became apparent that the policy would not solve the nation's fundamental social and economic problems. The Scottish economy had collapsed after 1918 with the post-war dislocation in the international economy. Demand for the traditional heavy capital investment goods which had powered the economy in the pre-war era dried up in an age of uncertainty. In addition to the traditional social problems which had plagued Scottish society (bad health, poor housing and poverty), the new phenomenon of long-term mass unemployment emerged. Labour's support for home rule in the pre-war era was conditioned by the belief that a Scottish parliament would be able to pursue radical social policies. Crucial to this idea was the notion that a parliament would have the power to redistribute resources.[8] Yet, as had become apparent to John Wheatley in the late twenties, Scottish society did not have the resources sufficient to the task. The solution to Scotland's endemic social and economic problems, he argued, could only be rectified by utilising the resources of the British state and empire.[9] It was this realisation which initiated Labour's *volte face* on home rule in the late twenties. The planned use of British state resources would remain the cardinal principle of Labour's unionism because economic and social salvation could only come from Westminster.

The Unionist Party displayed little interest in Labour's dalliance with home rule. As far as that party was concerned, Scottish nationalism

and home rule in the twenties was associateld with left-wing repub-
licanism, and other than outright denunciation, no special policy was
called for. The chill winds of the Great Depression in 1929, however,
forced a reassessment of the situation. The effects of the depression
were much greater north of the border, and in the onslaught against
the Scottish economy and society, traditional Unionist supporters
started to succumb to nationalist rhetoric.[10] The 'southward drift of
industry', rationalisation and statistic after statistic in the early thirties
showed that the Scots were bearing a disproportionate burden of
the crisis. Over-crowding in Scotland was six times greater than
England; there were more factory closures and less new factories
established; unemployment remained persistently higher than the
British average and social performance indicators, such as average
height and infant mortality rates, showed that the average Scot was
in much poorer physical shape than his southern counterpart.[11]
Traditional Unionist allies such as the Chambers of Commerce and
the press grumbled loudly about injustice to Scotland and the
Unionist Party even suffered a nationalist secession in Cathcart.[12]
Although Scottish nationalism never crystallised into an effective
political force in the inter-war period, the important point for the
development of Unionist strategy was the belief that it would.
Evidence of the jittery state of Unionist nerves is to be found in the
'Ragman's Roll': a public declaration by every titled person, every
prominent businessman and every public figure that the Unionists
could induce to give a public pledge that they were against Scottish
home rule. It was a rare public demonstration of the solidarity of the
Scottish establishment.[13]

The Unionist analysis of the causes of the nationalist unease and
sense of grievance was that it was fuelled by the depression. While
acknowledging that there was a legitimate sense of frustration,
Unionist politicians were wary of stoking the fires of nationalism.
This was especially the case when it was recognised that nationalism was in danger of spreading beyond its traditional boundary of
support among the 'cranks and romantics' into the territory of the
young, ambitious and practical. According to John Buchan, these were
the people who 'do a lot of the thinking of the nation' and Scottish
national sentiment would have to be appeased before it developed
into something altogether more sinister.[14] The problem facing the
Scottish Unionists, who made up the majority of the National
Government's political cohort in Scotland, was that there was little
they could do to solve the fundamental economic dislocation facing

Scottish society. Scottish industrialists pursued a 'wait and see' policy in the hope that things would pick up again.[15] The accepted economic orthodoxy was that government could do little to alter market forces and the policies of cheap credit, low interest and protectionism for the consumer durable industries, while of great benefit to the Tory heartland of the south, had little impact north of the border. Scottish industrial production in the thirties was smaller than the pre-war period and for many polemicists it seemed that the Scottish nation was locked into a process of terminal decline. According to George Malcolm Thomson: 'The first fact about the Scot is that he is a man eclipsed. The Scots are a dying race'.[16]

Unable to do little more than scratch the surface of Scottish economic problems, Unionist politicians were forced to use scare tactics to dampen down Scottish nationalism. While accepting that the Scottish economy was in considerable difficulty, it was argued that anything in the way of a severance or loosening of the ties with England would spell economic disaster. In short, if people believed that the situation was bad at the moment, it was nothing compared to the nationalist abyss of economic collapse which would be inevitable should the Scots opt for their own parliament. Prominent industrialists such as James Lithgow chimed in an anti-nationalist chorus that the precarious hold that Scottish industry had on its markets would be lost through political change.[17] Again and again, it was emphasised that Scotland needed England to survive. Whereas unionism in the pre-war era was strident and confident, in the inter-war period it had become defensive and negative. Sir Robert Horne, a former Chancellor of the Exchequer, berated his fellow countrymen for turning to nationalism and compared them unfavourably to the Welsh:

> The Welsh are showing the kind of wisdom that is generally attributed to the Scot, because, knowing that the amount of their unemployment is so much greater than elsewhere, probably they realise that they would find great difficulty in providing unemployment benefit by themselves, and they are wiser to rely on the richer country than to seek separation.[18]

Whatever the merits of this argument, it was not a confident espousal of the principles and benefits of unionism. For good measure, Bob Boothby, the Aberdeenshire MP, simultaneously claimed that while the Scots were capable of running the British Empire, it was a well known fact that left to its own devices, the Scottish nation would degenerate into barbarism.[19] In the thirties, the Union was increasingly portrayed less as mutually beneficial partnership between Scotland and England and more as a dependent relationship necessary for Scottish economic survival.

As a part of the ongoing process to diffuse the threat of nationalism and appease Scottish sentiment, the decision was taken to reform the government of Scotland in 1937. It was decided that the Scottish Office would be relocated in Edinburgh and that various arms of government policy should come under the umbrella of the power of the Secretary of State for Scotland. There were two objectives underlining this policy: the first was to create a powerful symbol of Scottish nationhood which would reinforce the notion that Scotland was a distinctive nation within the Union, and the second was to improve the apparatus of government in Scotland. Unionist politicians claimed that Scotland did not need more government in the shape of a parliament in Edinburgh, but rather better government.[20] Administrative devolution, it was believed, would bring government closer to the people and decisions taken about Scotland would now be taken in Scotland by Scots. It also had the advantage that it did not surrender political power, which would remain firmly in the hands of the National Government.[21] It was the apparent growth in the power of the Scottish Secretary of State which initiated renewed interest in Labour circles about Scottish home rule in the late thirties. Tom Johnston and others argued that the expansion of government in Scotland had occurred without any democratic checks and that government power was being abused for the political benefit of the Scottish Secretary and his industrialist allies.[22]

As well as the growth of a government apparatus in Scotland in the late thirties,there was also the planting of the seeds of corporatism which would flourish and develop during and after the Second World War. A whole host of committees and enquiries were undertaken into the state of the Scottish economy, most of which recommended greater state planning as a remedy for the structural imbalance of Scottish industry.[23] Also, various small scale developments such as the Hillington Industrial Estate and the Glasgow Empire Exhibition of 1938 were set up to encourage diversification, although few had any real impact. The real spur to state intervention in the Scottish economy in the late thirties, however, was rearmament which benefited the traditional industries and industrialists. In particular, shipbuilding was the prime beneficiary of an ever increasing state subsidy.[24] This was not lost on the critics of the National Government who complained bitterly at the state subsidising Scotland's traditional capitalist ruling class: 'Scotland has indeed been ruthlessly exploited and bled white, not by England, but her own industrialists'.[25] This was made especially poignant as the traditional industrialists were often the bitterest critics of state welfare.[26] Yet, as was pointed out by numerous commentators, rearmament would not solve Scotland's economic problems; it would merely put them on ice.

1939–1979: Tower Blocks, 'Pre-fabs' and 'New Towns'

Corporatism flourished in Scotland during the Second World War because the ground had been well prepared in the late thirties and also because it had a very keen proponent in the shape of Thomas Johnston, the Labour Party's wartime Secretary of State. The state was omnipresent in Scottish society during the war. It controlled what people made, where they worked, what they bought and what they ate. Johnston believed in consensus and sought to unite workers and employers in pursuit of war aims. He also trusted the 'experts' and made much of 'planning' for post-war reconstruction.[27] Another development during the war was the setting up of the Committee of Ex-Secretaries of State for Scotland to advise on future industrial and social policy. This was designed to pool together the best talent and best experience, although it is questionable if it had any real impact on future policy development.[28] The war had demonstrated the power of state action and there was a determination that this power should and would be harnessed for peacetime reconstruction. Although there was some flirting with the idea of Scottish home rule, most politicians had their eyes firmly fixed on the goal of using the regenerative powers of the British state. As was mentioned earlier, the principal reason why Labour had become attracted to the idea of setting up a parliament in Edinburgh during the thirties was due to a sense of exclusion from the state apparatus which was being constructed. The war, however, changed all that. With corporatism firmly enmeshed in the Scottish and British political psyche, it would no longer be acceptable to keep Labour out in the cold. Indeed, the actual experience of government in Scotland during the war had brought Labour firmly within the pale of government and Johnston demonstrated how remarkably effective it could be. Johnston's stewardship during the war actually posited an alternative strategy to home rule. His leadership revealed that it was not so much the system which was at fault during the thirties, but rather those who operated it. The 'strongman in the Cabinet' showed clearly that an able Scottish Secretary could wring concessions from Westminster and safeguard and promote Scottish interests.[29] When contrasted with the uncertainty of home rule, the proven ability to tap into the richer resources of the British state seemed for many a safer option. Furthermore, as social and economic planning was to be the watchword of future peacetime government, it made sense that this should be carried out at the strategically more important British level.

Scotland's peacetime prosperity was dependent on British state intervention and planning. The Clyde Valley Plan of 1946 (published in 1949) was a thorough-going proposal to diversify the Scottish economy away from its reliance on the traditional staples into new consumer durables. Plans for 'new towns' and the construction of a social infrastructure were part and parcel of the policy for the peacetime reconstruction of Scottish society. The Redistribution of Industries Act of 1945 and the Town and Country Planning Act of 1947 were designed to divert new industrial production away from the crowded and more prosperous areas of the south to those parts of the United Kingdom which needed them most. These acts were welcomed in Scotland because it was believed that the Scottish economy would be a prime beneficiary of such policies. The idea of the Welfare State and the planned economy caught the imagination and support of the Scottish public and politicians alike because there was, compared to other parts of the United Kingdom, more for the state to do. Yet the planners did not have it all their own way. The exigencies of Britain's post-war situation fatally wounded any prospect for a thorough-going transformation of the Scottish econ-omy. Strapped for cash by the cost of the war and the welfare reforms it was introducing, the Attlee government desperately needed export earnings. The Scottish economy was ideally placed to deliver this as the heavy industries supplied the needs of European and Imperial reconstruction.[30] In the short-term, this was of little consequence as the economy seemed to be booming and talk of attracting the aviation and car industries was dismissed as 'water over the dam' by a leading economist.[31] In any case, with full employment and a booming economy, the Cassandra type warnings of structural imbalance seemed to many, in retrospect, to have been over-played.

While the immediate post-war era appeared to be one of prosperity, by the late 1950s problems had begun to emerge. Rather than diversifying, Scottish dependence on the heavy industries was greater than it had been in the thirties. Productivity was poor and the economic growth rate of nine per cent was half that of the United Kingdom average for the period from 1954–60. Income per head of population was trailing thirteen per cent behind the British average.[32] The development of the consumer industry was achieved largely by attracting foreign companies, although only twenty four new factories opened in Scotland between 1946 and 1952.[33] The traditional industries seemed impervious to any notions of modernisation, with management and trade unions colluding to retain old labour intensive working practices. New investment which could have modernised traditional industries was shunned by both the public and private sectors. Government money was spent on attracting new industry. The Catto Report of 1952 highlighted the growing reliance of the Scottish economy on state subsidies and estimated that Scotland received about twelve per cent of government expenditure while only contributing ten per cent of revenue.[34] Deflation and public expenditure cuts in 1957, coupled with the ending of national service, meant that the jobless total in Scotland doubled between 1958 and 1959 to 116,000. Politicians and the electorate looked to the state for a remedy, and the solution offered to the problem of the Scottish economy in the Toothill Report of 1961 was for more planning and targeted regional assistance.[35] The connection between Scottish economic well-being and British state economic policy was now explicit.

The facilitation of such policies required a massive investment in the construction of a state apparatus. As a consequence, the existing arm of government in Scotland, the Scottish Office, expanded from 2,400 civil servants in 1937 to over 8,000 by 1970. The Balfour Report of 1953 recommended that wherever practical, the function of government in Scotland should be handled by the Scottish Office. Control of food, veterinary regulation, electricity, roads and bridges and health were transferred to the Scottish Secretary, all of which led to the creation of a separate and distinctive arm of government in Scotland. This enabled the Scottish Secretary to wield massive powers without direct accountability to the Scottish electorate. This was an administrative option favoured by both the Labour and Unionist parties and in the era of consensus politics, few voices were raised in concern as to the lack of democratic accountability.[36]

The social reconstruction of Scottish society was a key objective of the post-war Labour government and housing was high on its list of priorities. Although the problems of the economy proved particularly truculent, the British state was better equipped to deliver and meet the social welfare expectations of the Scottish population. Wartime bombing, poor repair work and the decline of privately rented accommodation were added to the inter-war problems of Scottish housing. From the outset of peace, it was clear that a major house building programme was required to meet the aspirations of both the people and the politicians. Given that the political consensus put the responsibility of social well-being on the state, most attention focused on council housing. The high standards demanded by the Labour governments, coupled with shortages of building materials, meant that initial progress was slow. In 1952 a further half a million houses were still required and more than fifty per cent of the existing stock had been built before 1900. Thirty per cent were still of two rooms or less and only twenty per cent had more than four rooms. This contrasted badly with England where less than five per cent were of two rooms or less and fifty per cent had four rooms or more.[37] The health service was still in embryonic form and only about six per cent of the total British local authority health care workers were employed in Scotland.[38] Tower blocks, 'pre-fabs' and 'new towns' were the 'pragmatic' solutions offered by experts and favoured by the incoming Conservative administrations after 1951. Not only were such schemes more economical, they were the only way in which the government could realise its political priority of meeting rehousing targets. The scale of building was impressive, with 38,000 constructed in 1954 alone.

Housing construction was, however, subject to competing political claims, reflecting the different interest groups which developed in response to the growth of the corporate state in Scotland. The Scottish Office, local councils and local politicians, all used their influence to further their own interests, often with little regard for the interests of residents. Relations between Glasgow District Council and the Scottish Special Housing Association, for example, were generally at arms length and distinctly frosty, as local government jealously protected its territory against the encroachments of central government.[39] Local councillors and MPs stamped their own peculiar brands of teetotalism and anti-capitalism onto housing estates by denying outlets for shops and pubs. Planners exercised their middle-class utopian social idealism on pliant working-class communities,

although it would take a decade before the disastrous social consequences of such pipe dreams came home to roost. Full employment
brought relative prosperity to the Scottish nation in the 1950s and
the gap in the wages differential with England narrowed for a time.
The impact of the Health Service and increased purchasing power
led to a marked improvement in the nation's health. Infant mortality
rates decreased, the average height of children increased and people
were living to an older age. Although nationalism rumbled on in
various quarters, few questioned the efficacy of British state planning
as a means to safe-guard the nation's social and economic well-being.

Scottish politics in the fifties and sixties were dominated by the
ability of the British state to deliver social and economic prosperity
and unsurprisingly, the ebb and flow of party fortunes closely
reflected those of the United Kingdom. In the general elections
between and including 1950 and 1964, the Unionists averaged 46
per cent of the vote while Labour averaged 47 per cent. Above all else
it was the vagaries of the 'first past the post' electoral system which
accounted for the loss and gain of seats. Political success in Scotland
was dependent, as it was in the United Kingdom, on the ability of
parties to present themselves as the most capable candidate for
managing government. Although there was little difference between
the Unionists and Labour, either in terms of the share of votes or
parliamentary seats won, the Unionists can be said to have been
most successful, given that the Scottish social structure was more
inclined towards traditional Labour voters. The appeal to a consumer
society in the general election of 1951 contrasted favourably with
Labour's record of rationing, controls and austerity. Also, the
Unionists made a great play on the belief that Labour's policy of
nationalisation and centralisation was removing control from
Scotland and harming Scottish national interests.[40] By the late
fifties, however, the persistent sluggishness of the Scottish economy
and the raised expectations of its workforce meant that the Scots
were more receptive to Harold Wilson's brighter promises and
slick presentation of his greater expertise in the field of economic
management in the general election of 1964. The Labour Party's
commitment to the 'white heat of technology' and a greater and
improved role for the corporate state seduced many Scottish voters.

Wilson's Labour governments of the sixties embarked on an
ambitious project of state sponsored economic expansion north of
the border. The Highlands and Islands Development Board and
regional economic boards were created to facilitate a massive public

expenditure programme which was designed to build up the economic infrastructure by concentrating on health, housing, transport and education.[41] Job creation was a central component of this strategy and it was believed that the resultant employment from the construction of, and to a lesser extent the staffing of, these programmes would not only offset predicted job losses in the struggling heavy industries, but would also attract consumer industries which would be lured north by the prospect of a buoyant market based on full employment. Planning was more or less handicapped from the outset. Labour's fifteen seat lead in Scotland at the general election of 1964 secured the Labour government's seven seat majority in the House of Commons. Economic planning was sacrificed on the altar of political expediency especially after 1967, when the Scottish National Party (SNP) won a by-election from Labour. The Scottish Secretary, William Ross, mercilessly used the danger of a nationalist upsurge to screw more money out of the Cabinet and by the late sixties government expenditure per head in Scotland was running at twenty per cent above the British average.[42] Bad industrial relations, poor and inexperienced planning and planners, wild optimism, oscillating levels of public expenditure and short-term political calculations all combined to produce a catalogue of economic failure. The attainment of the social objectives of full employment and a prosperous society were increasingly dependent on high levels of government expenditure. The more the Scottish economy failed to diversify and attract new industry and services, the more it relied on government and the more this determined political behaviour.

It was the failure of the London government in the late sixties and early seventies which propelled the SNP to the centre of the British political stage. The success of the SNP in the Hamilton by-election of 1967 taught the Scottish electorate a valuable lesson: a nationalist vote was the most efficient means of making the British state take Scottish aspirations and grievances seriously. While British politicians oscillated in their commitment to a Scottish parliament, the preferred option was to address the social and economic problems which were thought to be giving rise to nationalist discontent.[43] Ted Heath, for example, pledged the Conservative Party to a Scottish Assembly in 1968, but his government of the early seventies ignored this and instead increased state expenditure.[44] The Labour governments of the seventies faced the most serious nationalist challenge. Although the SNP was able to capture thirty per cent of the vote in the second general election of 1974, opinion poll evidence tends to suggest that the party benefited primarily from the protest vote as most supporters did not endorse the nationalist flagship policy of independence. At a time of mounting economic crisis and comparative social and economic under-achievement, many Scots looked to an increased nationalist political presence as the best way to wring further concessions from Westminster. Indeed, while Labour tried to cobble together a coherent devolutionist package in the face of strong internal opposition, further tried and trusted methods of Scottish appeasement continued. More economic power was devolved to the Scottish Office, principally through the establishment of the Scottish Development Agency. Although the Cabinet records are not yet available for public scrutiny, Labour's timing on devolution in the seventies does appear to be significant. The financial crisis which led the Chancellor of the Exchequer, Dennis Healey, to go cap in hand to the International Monetary Fund resulted in a stringent pruning of public finances. Thereafter, devolution emerged as the best means of appeasing Scottish national sentiment in the absence of greater state resources.

Further evidence that corporatism remained at the heart of Scottish political aspirations in the seventies can be found in the devolution referendum of 1979 and the subsequent general election. Although a majority of Scots voted for an Assembly, the Cunningham amendment meant that because less than forty per cent of the total eligible electorate endorsed devolution, it would not be enacted. For many Scots, then and since, this fiasco has been seen as an unfair ploy which denied the Scots their legitimate devolutionist aspiration. Yet, the truth of the matter is that the majority was extremely narrow – less than three per cent – and the issue divided Scottish society more than it united it. Furthermore, in the general election of 1979 there was a move away from the SNP back to the Labour Party, which revealed the British state corporatist loyalties of many former nationalist voters. In any case, the issue died away in the early eighties, which again is evidence of the fact that the nationalist upsurge of the seventies was motivated by a desire to protest at the failure of London government to meet the aspirations of the Scottish post-war consensus. It was not an indictment or rejection of those aspirations.

1979–1997: 'In short, Scotland was subsidised.'

The longevity of corporatism in Scottish political culture is one factor which helps to explain why the Conservative Party has lost so much support in Scotland since 1979. Although the experience of the planned economy and the Welfare State was a mixed bag of results for Scottish society, on the whole, most people thought that it worked. The Thatcherite attack on corporatism and the 'nanny state' was unacceptable to many Scots because the state had been such a well spring of Scottish social and economic well-being since 1945. Furthermore, given the extended range of state activity in Scotland compared to the Tory heartland of the south, it was easy for the Scottish electorate to confuse an attack on the corporate state as an attack against the Scottish nation. In any case, the dismantling of the 'nanny state' was going to have a greater effect on the Scots because there was more to dismantle. Clearly such moves would have dramatic implications for Conservative support.

Nationalism again emerged in Scottish politics, this time not because of the failings of the corporate state, but because of a perception of an external attack on the system. Paradoxically, the defence of such British institutions as the social security system and the health service, increasingly took on a nationalist air. As has been argued throughout this piece, the growth of corporatism and state welfarism were central to a redefinition of Britishness which the Scots could accept after the traumatic experience of social and economic dislocation in the inter-war era. Yet the Thatcher revolution of the eighties undermined what was for many Scots the true essence of a British identity and political loyalty. The Thatcherite electoral hegemony robbed the Scots of this form of British identity and the values of corporatism and state intervention were, as a consequence, increasingly represented as belonging to a distinct Scottish political culture.

A further paradox emerges when examining the Conservative response to the perceived upsurge in nationalist support engendered by the attack on the 'nanny state'. Political independence was dismissed by the Conservative Party and others as idle day-dreaming because an independent Scotland could not economically support itself. Conservative Secretaries of State took great delight in publishing figures which showed that per head of population, Scotland received a disproportionate share of identifiable public expenditure.[45] In short, Scotland was subsidised. This theme was reiterated by the Labour Party. Yet it was more damaging to the Conservative Party, because traditional middle-class voters do not like being told that they are 'spongers'. Indeed, as the social profile of Scotland has become increasingly similar to that of England since the eighties, political behaviour has diverged. (Clearly, arguments rooted in structural analyses of Scottish society or class systems are inadequate as explanations of this phenomenon.) Furthermore, the Conservative Party appeared to be saying different things in Scotland and England. South of the border there was great emphasis on standing on your own feet with no state support and independence was praised as great virtue. North of the border the message was that Scotland could not stand on its own and that independence was unfeasible. It was a 'catch twenty two' situation. The notion of 'subsidy junkies' was politically offensive, but it was needed to deal with the threat of nationalism. The more the corporate state was dismantled, the more Conservative unpopularity grew and the more Scottish politics took on a nationalist air. The greater the nationalist tinge in Scottish politics, the more the Conservatives felt the need to emphasis Scottish subsidisation.

Conclusion

In conclusion, British politicians in Scotland have pragmatically used the resources of the British state to further their own interests. The Union has been presented as an opportunity for Scots to gain more than they put in. Also, it has been presented as the guarantor of social and economic well-being. This has been done negatively, as in the case of the inter-war period when the Scots were told that they needed England to survive, or positively, in the case of the period from 1945–70, when the Scots were encouraged to expect the British state to improve and protect their standard of living. Since 1979, British political culture has rejected the centrality of the state as the principal means to ensure social and economic well-being and unionism has increasingly relied on negative assumptions of Scottish dependency as its central intellectual vindication. Either positively or negatively, unionism in the twentieth century has been largely based on Scottish dependency.

NOTES

1. James Mitchell, 'Scotland in the Union, 1945–95: the Changing Nature of the Union State' in T. M. Devine and R. J. Finlay (eds), *Scotland in the Twentieth Century*, (Edinburgh, 1996), p. 98.
2. R. J. Finlay, *A Partnership for Good? Scottish Politics and the Union Since 1880*, (Edinburgh, 1997), pp. 134–45.
3. *Ibid.*, pp. 93–115.

4. R. J. Finlay, 'The Rise and Fall of Popular Imperialism in Scotland, 1850–1950', *Scottish Geographical Magazine*, 113 (1997), pp. 13–21.
5. *Scotsman*, 4 Dec. 1906.
6. Finlay, *Partnership for Good?*, pp. 41–69.
7. R. J. Finlay, 'National Identity in Crisis? Politicians, Intellectuals and the "End of Scotland", 1918–39', *History*, 79 (1994), pp. 242–59.
8. Finlay, *Partnership for Good?*, pp. 51–67.
9. David Howell, *A Lost left: Three Studies in Socialism and Nationalism*, (Manchester, 1986), pp. 229–65.
10. Finlay, 'National Identity in Crisis?', p. 245.
11. *Ibid.*
12. *Daily Record*, 22 March 1932.
13. R. J. Finlay, *Independent and Free: Scottish Politics and the Origins of the Scottish National Party, 1918–45*, (Edinburgh, 1994), p. 93.
14. *H[ouse of] C[ommons Parliamentary] Deb[ate]s (Third Series)*, Vol. 272, col. 262, 22 Nov. 1932.
15. R. H. Campbell, *The Rise and Fall of Scottish Industry*, (Edinburgh, 1983), pp. 133–64.
16. G. M. Thomson, *Caledonia or the Future of the Scots*, (London, 1927), p. 63.
17. *Daily Record*, 20 Oct. 1932.
18. *H.C. Debs*, Vol. 272, col. 265, 22 Nov. 1932.
19. *The Nation*, 9 March 1929.
20. John Buchan, *H.C. Debs*, Vol. 272, col. 265, 22 Nov. 1932.
21. James Mitchell, *Conservatives and the Union: A Survey of Conservative Party Attitudes to Scotland*, (Edinburgh, 1990), pp. 17–26.
22. Thomas Burns, *Self-Government for Scotland*, (Glasgow, 1937).
23. See, for example, the annual *Clydesdale Bank Report of the Scottish Economy*; James Bowie, *The Future of Scotland*, (Edinburgh, 1939); G. M. Thomson, *Scotland : That Distressed Area*, (Edinburgh, 1935); *Report by the University of Glasgow into the Problems of the Scottish Economy*, (Glasgow, 1937), *Scottish Economic Committee, Scotland's Industrial Future: The Case for Planned Development*, (London, 1939).
24. Board of Trade, *Survey of Production*, (London, 1935–39).
25. T. Burns, *A Plan for Scotland*, (Perth, 1937), p. 24.
26. T. Burns, *The Real Rulers of Scotland*, (Glasgow, 1940).
27. G. Walker, *Thomas Johnston*, (Manchester, 1988), pp. 158–77.
28. R. H. Campbell, 'The Committee of Ex-Secretaries of State for Scotland and Industrial Policy, 1941–45', *Scottish Industrial History*, 2 (1981), pp. 3–11.
29. Chris Harvie, 'Labour and Scottish Government: The Age of Tom Johnston', *The Bulletin of Scottish Politics*, (Spring, 1981), pp. 1–20.
30. R. Saville 'The Industrial Background to the Post-War Scottish Economy' in R. Saville (ed.), *The Economic Development of Modern Scotland, 1950–80*, (Edinburgh, 1985), pp. 1–47.
31. Alec Cairncross, *Scotsman*, 24 Oct. 1952.
32. See Saville (ed.), *Economic Development of Modern Scotland*.
33. *Scotsman*, 4 Dec. 1952.
34. *Report on the Scottish Financial and Trade Statistics* Cmnd. 8609 (London, 1952).

35. J. N. Toothill, *Report on the Scottish Economy*, (Edinburgh, 1961).
36. I. G. C. Hutchison, 'Government' in Devine and Finlay (eds), *Scotland in the Twentieth Century*, pp. 46–64.
37. Statistics taken from the *Scotsman*, 4 December 1952.
38. *Ibid.*, 4 December 1952.
39. Hutchison, 'Government', p. 58.
40. *Scottish Control: Scottish Affairs: Unionist Policy*, (Glasgow, 1948).
41. G. McCrone, *Regional Policy in Britain*(London, 1970), pp. 106–20.
42. G. McCrone, 'The Role of Government' in Saville (ed.), *Economic Development of Modern Scotland*, pp. 195–213.
43. Finlay, *Partnership for Good?*, pp. 146–64.
44. Mitchell, 'Scotland and the Union', p. 95.
45. This is an issue which is surrounded by much controversy. Identifiable expenditure is only what the government chooses to identify and is not the total sum of government expenditure. Unidentifiable expenditure accounts for perhaps as much as twenty five per cent of the total and includes mortgage tax relief, rates relief and research and development, very little of which come to Scotland. See C. H. Lee, *Scotland and the United Kingdom: The Economy and the Union in the Twentieth Century*, (Manchester, 1995), pp. 129–53; and A. Midwinter, M. Keating & J. Mitchell, *Politics and Public Policy in Scotland*, (London, 1991), pp. 119–38.

7

CONTEMPORARY UNIONISM

James Mitchell

What is Unionism?

Unionism is a term which is used loosely and its meaning is highly contested. To some, unionism suggests a reactionary disposition and dogmatic opposition to reform. To others, unionism means support for well established and successful institutions and opposition to threats to the integrity of the state. In any attempt to understand contemporary unionism, it is important to take account of its popular and contested uses but also to go beyond these. If it has any merit as a social science term or analytical tool, then some objective meaning of unionism needs to be found, categories of unionism need to be distinguished, and the concept applied to contemporary politics.

Unionism is essentially a form of nationalism, in the sense that it is the ideology which favours the territorial integrity of the state. This definition is necessarily vague in order to cope with the variety of unionisms which can be identified. Different categories of unionism can be discerned which flesh it out. The notion that unionism is a form of nationalism draws on the definition of the latter which sees the state as an 'imagined community'. It is imagined 'because the members of even the smallest nation will never know most of their fellow-members, meet them, or even hear of them, yet in the minds of each lives the image of their community.' It is a community because 'regardless of the actual inequality and exploitation that may prevail in each, the nation is always conceived as a deep, horizontal comradeship.'[1]

Keating has distinguished between state and regional nationalisms. Unionism is a form of state nationalism – ideological allegiance to the existing state. Challenges to the state from nationalisms within the state would come from regional nationalisms.[2] A similar distinction is made by Kellas when he refers to ethnic, social and official nationalisms.[2] Ethnic nationalism is 'exclusive' as it excludes from membership anyone not sharing a common ethnicity. Social nationalism is more open and 'inclusive'. Official nationalism is the 'nationalism of the state' and, as such, is similar to Keating's idea of state nationalism.[3] Whether state or official nationalism is ethnic or social, exclusive or inclusive, is an open question. Discussions of this sort usually focus on citizenship: who is entitled to belong to the state. Exclusive nationalisms are unwilling to open their borders to those born beyond them and set strict criteria for membership. Inclusive nationalisms are more open and welcoming. Equally, this distinction could be used to consider the state's attitude to its own citizenry. Unionism, as state nationalism, takes both forms: it can be exclusive or it can be inclusive. An exclusive state nationalism is assimilationist, unwilling to countenance diversity whether in terms of race, religion, ethnicity or some other characteristic. An inclusive nationalism is open and pluralistic, viewing membership and identification with the all-embracing state and nation as fully compatible with other identities. An exclusive British nationalism is one which would frown upon Scottish, Welsh, Hindu or Muslim identities. An inclusive British nationalism would see Britishness as compatible with being Scottish or being a Muslim, for example.

Unionism, as nationalism, rarely rates a mention in text books on British politics. As Rose has written, there is not even a collective noun for citizens of the UK:[4]

> Trying to name the nation associated with the government of the United Kingdom displays the confusion about national identity. One thing is certain: no one speaks of the 'UKes' as a nation.[5]

The absence of a collective noun, however, should not be confused with the absence of a United Kingdom national identity. It may be confused and at times be described as British when 'UK-ish' is meant, but identification with the state and, more importantly, with the people constituting the state exists. As Billig has noted, state nationalism is daily 'reproduced in a banally mundane way'.[6] In political discourse in the UK, nationalism is generally taken to refer to 'regional nationalisms' challenging the state, to Scottish, Welsh or Irish nationalisms. However, the absence of references in academic texts to UK nationalism does not mean that it is weak. If anything, this signals its strength. UK nationalism is taken for granted to such an extent that it is often seen as part of the natural order. Only in times when the state is threatened – usually from outside rather than from within – do we tend to see the term nationalism used with reference to the UK as a whole. In recent years, the UK state nationalism has become increasingly recognised in dealings with the European Union.

Whether states create nations or nations create states is an empirical question. In the case of Germany, and more so Italy, the state preceded the nation.[7] After the establishment of the Italian state in 1860, D'Azeglio, a leader of the *Risorgimento*, famously remarked, 'We have made Italy, now we must make Italians.' After the state was formed, the process of 'nation-building' had to begin. The process of nation-building involves winning the acceptance and legitimacy of new states which are created through the combination of different communities or nations. The creation of states 'involves first the acquisition of territory, then the imposition of authority within it.'[8] There was a determined effort on the part of state governments to create 'Italians' and 'Germans' after the establishment of Italy and Germany. Also, through universal education, military service and improved communications, the French state attempted to turn 'peasants into Frenchmen' after 1870.[9] The latter involved a process of acculturation: 'the civilisation of the French by urban France, the disintegration of local cultures by modernity and their absorption into the dominant civilisation of Paris and the schools.'[10]

State nationalism in the UK has been quite different from that found in other parts of Europe. There was little comparable 'nation-building' of this sort in the UK. Instead Colley has identified a number of forces which helped 'forge the nation' of Britain between 1707 and 1837.[11] However, though nation-building may have been a consequence of war, colonialism and Protestantism, it was not a primary objective. The lack of a conscious British nation-building project is notable.

Universal education in Britain began to emerge in the nineteenth century. However, from the provision of central government grants in the early part of the century through to the establishment of central administration to administer and govern the growth in state education later, Scotland was treated as a separate entity. Not only was there no attempt to eradicate 'local cultures', but the state insulated them from other homogenising forces such as industrialisation and urbanisation. Whether wittingly or not, a sense of state nationalism was probably imparted through the teaching of history and geography with particular reference to the British Empire. The

Empire was always referred to as the *British* Empire, but it was a dual notion of Britishness. The Scots had their place within the British Empire as Scots. Military service existed, and while this played its part in forging the nation, it also permitted a dual sense of identity through the existence of Scottish regiments. The structure of government which operated also allowed for this duality. Scottish central administration was quite distinct with a system of boards based in Edinburgh which were replaced by 1939 by the Scottish Office. Just as it would be wrong to talk about a Scottish Empire or a Scottish army, there was *no* Scottish government. But equally, the British Empire, British army and British government had their Scottish components.

The state catered for Scottish distinctiveness and even encouraged a dual identity. The duality, however, was lopsided. The state was unambiguously the United Kingdom and it was a function of its strength that it could permit Scottish institutions and a sense of Scottish identity to exist within it. If the state had been threatened or weakened, as it was to be a century later, then state nationalism could change and become more exclusive, less pluralistic. The duality was unusual but it should not be exaggerated. It was contingent on the success or perceived success of the state.

Unionism in the UK can therefore be seen as more than an ideology – it has been a process of nation-building. It has been unusual in that it has been more inclusive, more pluralistic than many other state nationalisms. Any understanding of unionism as a nation-building process today requires some appreciation of its origins and development. This legacy has been important. As will be shown below, the pluralistic base was threatened at different times and by different forces over the post-war period. As has always been the case, the nature of the state and consequently the nature of state nationalism has changed over time. The dynamic property both of state development and continuous nation-building is evident in all states. What makes the UK unusual is that the framework within which debates on the territorial organisation of the state and the nature of unionism take place is more fluid, given the absence of an entrenched, written constitution.

Unionism as Constitutional Conservatism

One important division within unionism concerns strategy: how the union should be maintained. Unionism is essentially a conservative ideology. Michels identified two chief uses of the term 'conservatism'. The first pointed to a 'tendency to maintain the status quo regardless of what may be' and the second had a more philosophical meaning, implying a 'particular *Weltanschauung*, such as love of authority and tradition'.[12] Unionism is conservatism of the first sort and is largely devoid of philosophical content. As with Conservatism, there are disputes within unionism as to what should be conserved and how best it should be conserved. The issue of what is fundamental and must be preserved at all costs will be disputed by unionists as well as the nature, extent and timing of change.

Alex Salmond, current leader of the Scottish National Party (SNP), is fond of pointing out that his Labour opponents argue that the union is in danger if a devolved Parliament is not set up, while some of his Conservative opponents argue that devolution will endanger the union. To some extent, these claims reflect the heated rhetoric of the devolution debate, but some unionist opponents and some unionist supporters of devolution honestly believe that the union is in danger if their preferred path is not followed. Both the unionist devolutionist and the unionist anti-devolutionist claim to wish to preserve the union. It is possible that they agree on objectives but disagree on how to go about achieving them. But equally, it is possible that behind the shared rhetoric of 'saving the union' lie quite different conceptions of what this means.

Some devolutionists prefer to present devolution as a pragmatic readjustment of the British state rather than a radical change.[13] This may simply be an attempt to make devolution more palatable to a timid electorate. Whether unionist devolutionists have more in common with unionist anti-devolutionists or with Scottish nationalists depends on more than language. In the 1970s, the main reason for Labour's 'U-turn' on devolution, when it moved from opposing the policy to supporting it, was the electoral threat posed by the SNP. Twenty years on the SNP is more of a threat but less significant in Labour's commitment to devolution.[14] Labour support for devolution in the 1970s was reactive, more about saving the Union (or at least Labour seats), but it has since become more positive. For Conservatives, however, it would appear that the opposite has occurred. Conservative equivocation on devolution in the 1970s suggested that the party did not view devolution as necessarily a threat to the integrity of the state. However, its rhetoric and outright opposition to devolution in the 1992 and 1997 general elections suggests that many have come to view devolution as the 'slippery slope to separatism', to use the phrase frequently used by anti-devolutionists in the 1979 referendum campaign.[15]

There is now a deeper divide within unionism than in the past. Unionist supporters of devolution see it in terms similar to the SNP view of independence. Self-government, rather than unionism, is the motivation and language of devolutionists. The 'Claim of Right', signed by almost all Labour MPs and all Liberal Democrat MPs in 1989, is a document which argues for reform of the state but uses strikingly nationalist language and arguments. It is Scotland's 'right' which is being asserted.

Unionists and Assimilationists

The creation of Britain with the 'merger' of England and Scotland in 1707 is important in understanding contemporary unionism in two respects. State formation plays a significant part in most states' future constitutional development. The original basis of any state may wither in time, but it remains the starting point. In addition, in the British case the absence of a formalised written constitution has meant that the settlement bringing the new state into being is given greater importance than might be the case otherwise. It has been argued, for example, that the Treaty of Union is not like other acts of Parliament but rather represents a form of fundamental law. In other words, it performs a similar function to a written constitution or a 'particular set of constituent provisions' similar to that involved in establishing the United States of America.[16] Though Scottish nationalists rather than unionists have been most active in articulating this viewpoint, there is much sympathy for it amongst unionists, at least amongst one branch of unionism.

A distinction made in a study, of state formation is useful when applied to the study of contemporary unionism.[17] Rokkan and Urwin distinguished between unitary and union state formations:

> The *unitary state*, built up around one unambiguous political centre which enjoys economic dominance and pursues a more or less undeviating policy of administrative standardisation. All areas of the state are treated alike, and all institutions are directly under the control of the centre.

> The *union state*, not the result of straightforward dynastic conquest. Incorporation of at least parts of its territory has been achieved through personal dynastic union, for example by treaty, marriage or

inheritance. Integration is less than perfect. While administrative standardisation prevails over most of the territory, the consequences of personal union entail the survival in some areas of pre-union rights and institutional infrastructures which preserve some degree of regional autonomy and serve as agencies of indigenous elite recruitment.

A union state interpretation is a pluralist interpretation and more accurate historically, whereas a unitary state interpretation views power as more centralised. The implications of viewing the state as a union or unitary state are significant for contemporary politics, not just for an understanding of the creation of the modern state.

This distinction can be viewed either as interpretative or prescriptive. The UK could be interpreted as either a unitary or a union state in its foundation or as it has developed. Increasingly, historians and social scientists appreciate that the UK was originally and largely remains a union state, though this may not be the term used. Prescriptively, unionists may want it to become more assimilationist (conforming to the unitary state model) or maintain, reform or enhance its union state features.

The interpretative and prescriptive distinctions will usually be related. It is probable that unionists who believe the UK is a unitary state will oppose reform while those who see it as a union state will support reform. Prescriptive supporters of a union state might best be described as unionist while prescriptive supporters of a unitary state might best be described as assimilationists. Before the Second World War there were few assimilationists active in British politics. The assimilationist tendency has grown in post-war British politics.

The distinction between unionists and assimilationists is important and is particularly useful in understanding changes within the Conservative Party over the last twenty years. However, a distinction needs to be drawn between different types of prescriptive unionists. Especially over the course of the twentieth century a substantial gap has opened up within unionism. While agreement remains on the need to cater for Scottish distinctiveness, considerable differences have emerged on how this is best achieved. The gulf within unionism is such that at one extreme some unionists appear to have more in common with assimilationists, while at the other, they appear to have more in common with Scottish nationalists. Indeed, it is becoming increasingly difficult to justify the use of the term unionist for such a heterogeneous group. It will be argued below that the key divide in constitutional politics is no longer marked out by terms such as assimilationist/unionist/regional/nationalist, but rather that the key divide lies somewhere within the unionist camp and that new terms at least in discussing political prescriptions are needed.

Conservatives and Unionism

Unionism is often seen as synonymous with the Conservative Party in Scottish politics. This is understandable as the Conservatives alone remain, to a certain extent, hostile to a Scottish Parliament. In addition, the Conservatives were officially called the Scottish Unionist Party between 1912 and 1965 and since 1965 have officially called themselves the Scottish Conservative and Unionist Party.[18] The changes of name reflected the changing context of Scottish politics. The original insertion of Unionism into the party title had nothing to do with the Anglo-Scottish Union, rather the Union with Ireland was what was being referred to. There were a number of consequences for Scottish Unionism as a result.

Unionism, as the philosophy of Scottish Conservatives, had three meanings: a social and cultural meaning, a political economy meaning, and a constitutional meaning. Its social and cultural meaning came from the new support, especially with an extended franchise, which the party attracted as a consequence of supporting continued union with Ireland. This meant that the party had a more working-class appearance and culture, especially in the west of Scotland, than it might otherwise have had. As McFarland makes clear elsewhere in this volume, Protestantism and links with the Orange Order became important parts of the Scottish Unionist Party's identity. Opposition to Irish Catholic immigration became an important part of the party's platform – at least rhetorically – even though the wilder, sectarian elements were generally restrained. It was not simply a party of the upper classes. This had implications for Unionism's political economy. The party could not simply be the voice of one class. With a substantial section of working class supporters, the party had to take some account of the needs of this section of the electorate. It is little surprise to find some Scottish Unionist Party politicians adopting views to the left of mainstream British Conservatism.

In terms of constitutional politics, Ireland's constitutional status was important to the Scottish Unionist Party and remained an important part of its ethos even after Ireland broke away from

Britain. But the party consistently acknowledged that Scotland had a distinct position within Britain. The Scottish Unionist Party was not the Conservative Party and Scotland was not England. Strong support was shown for maintaining Scottish distinctiveness and occasional support for Scottish home rule was evident from some members. A unionist state form of unionism – traditional unionism – dominated Scottish Unionist thinking throughout its existence. Unionism, as state nationalism, was under no threat and Britain was perceived to be successful. The state was providing both the material and psychic incomes of British nationalism.[19] Especially in the immediate post-war period, the sense of British pride was at its height. Britain had won the war during which, albeit for a very short period, it had stood alone against Nazi Germany. The welfare state which emerged gave Scots good reason to feel attached to the state. Indeed, arguably it has been the welfare state, rather than a British or Scottish state, for which Scots have shown most consistent support.[20]

The conflict between assimilationist and traditional unionist positions has become more evident within the Conservative Party over the last twenty years. The UK as a union state fitted well with a Conservative outlook and distaste for uniformity and rationalism and a preference for tradition and the 'organic' nature of politics.[21] Not only did Conservatives accept the lack of symmetry which was the hallmark of the union state, they praised this, seeing it as part of the state and their party's heritage. Perceived threats to this established order were attacked by Conservatives. A key theme of Conservative attacks on the Labour Party was its 'ultra-rationalism'. Labour was presented as attempting to impose uniformity across the state. The argument that equality meant uniformity was extended to the field of constitutional politics.

A number of public and party documents provide evidence of traditional unionism. From the Report of the Gilmour Committee on Scottish Administration,[22] established by the Conservatives to investigate Scottish central administration in the 1930s, through to Ian Lang and Barry Henderson's pamphlet on the history of the Scottish Tories, the party expressed itself in terms of traditional unionism.[23] Tapping Scottish nationalist sentiment by arguing that their chief opponent was anti-Scottish was as much a feature of Conservative campaigning in the immediate post-war period as it was to become a feature of Labour attacks on the Conservatives in the 1980s.

A change 'set in' after Margaret Thatcher became party leader in 1975. An assimilationist strand emerged in Scottish Conservative thinking which challenged many of the old traditional unionist assumptions. Scotland's distinct status was questioned. The most notable example of this phenomenon concerned the Scottish Office, emblematic of traditional unionism. As Richard Finlay explains elsewhere in this volume, Margaret Thatcher held the much lauded spending powers of the Scottish office in contempt. Other examples of the assimilationist tendency included the questioning of Scottish 'over-representation' in Parliament. The Conservative Party officially supported a reduction in Scottish representation at Westminster and demands for a reduction in Scottish public expenditure, which led in 1992 to a change in the formula to Scotland's disadvantage.[24]

There are a number of different explanations for this, reflecting the debates on the nature of Thatcherism.[25] Margaret Thatcher's abrasive personality and her ideology may have played a part, but more significant was the context of British economic decline and its associated electoral considerations. The former led to public expenditure constraints and an attempt to 'rein in' institutions and groups which were perceived to be making excessive and unfair demands. This included Scotland and the Scottish Office. The latter meant that Conservatives concentrated their attentions on their electoral heartlands and pivotal, electoral regions of Britain. Thatcher's 'statecraft', the 'art of winning elections and achieving some necessary degree of governing competence in office',[26] left Scotland out in the cold and spawned an assimilationist tendency.

The electoral consequences of Thatcherism's assimilationist tendencies may have helped the Conservative Party win elections and govern Britain, but it had long-term costs. The Scottish Conservative vote and number of Scottish Tory MPs and councillors declined, and the party was attacked by its opponents for its anti-Scottish outlook. Though this kind of jibe had always been used to some extent by opponents of any party when in government, it proved more potent in the 1980s against the Conservatives. The electorate proved remarkably receptive to the message. By the 1987 and 1992 elections, Conservatives were having great difficulty winning support amongst people in Scotland who identified themselves as Scottish or more Scottish than British. Though they were doing well amongst those who saw themselves as British or more British than Scottish, this was a much smaller element in the electorate.[27] Once the image began to stick, the Conservatives had problems holding onto their vote. Moreover, the more they lost votes and seats, the more they looked as if they were governing Scotland against the will of the Scots. The 1987 election resulted in a sharp fall in Conservative fortunes in Scotland. The party lost ten seats and 4.4 per cent of the vote.

The departure of Margaret Thatcher offered the Scottish Conservatives an opportunity to alter their image. John Major and Ian Lang, his new Secretary of State for Scotland, made efforts to make the party appear more sympathetic to the Scottish dimension, but their's was a rather half-hearted effort to re-assert traditional unionism. During the 1992 election, Major agreed to 'take stock' of Scotland's status in the event of another Conservative victory. The 'stock taking' exercise was a very superficial exercise. A number of 'eminent' Scots, chosen for reasons that remain obscure, had a well publicised meeting with Major. It was more successful as an exercise in public relations than as one of public consultation. After a number of postponements a white paper was issued, 'Scotland in the Union: a partnership for good.'[28] In tone, it imitated earlier such documents, but in substance it was a pale reflection. The lack of new ideas and Lang's inability to generate much interest in the matter seemed to suggest that the Tories had lost interest in developing and reviving traditional unionism.

The appointment of Michael Forsyth in July 1995, however, suggested that the Scottish Tories were far from being a spent force, at least in terms of ideas and energy. Forsyth had been the party's chairman from July 1989 until October 1990. During this period he had the strong backing of Margaret Thatcher but was in almost constant conflict with Malcolm Rifkind, then Secretary of State for Scotland, and other senior members of the party north of the border. After a year, Thatcher removed Forsyth from the chairmanship while simultaneously promoting him within the Government. The former signalled the pressure on her to get rid of him from senior Tories, while the latter signalled her personal faith in him. Forsyth 're-invented' himself on his appointment to the Scottish Office in 1995. He adopted a more conciliatory approach in internal party matters and attempted to project himself as a Scottish Minister. Most remarkable was the launch of the first serious campaign against devolution from within the Conservative Party since 1979. Forsyth focused on the tax-varying powers of the Scottish Parliament proposed by the Scottish Constitutional Convention – a cross-party initiative which involved the Labour and Liberal Democrat parties, trade unions, churches and local authorities. The 'tartan tax' jibe did not have the same rhetorical power which the 'poll tax' had, but it caused 'New' Labour, determined to get rid of its 'tax-and-spend' image, many problems.

In 1995, signs that old-style unionism was being reborn were evident when a kilted Forsyth attended the premiere of 'Braveheart', a Hollywood production of the story of William Wallace. The following summer, Forsyth announced that the Stone of Destiny would be returned to Scotland.[29] The Stone was ceremoniously returned to Scotland on St Andrew's Day, 1996. A few months later Forsyth criticised the lack of knowledge of Scottish history amongst young Scots and set in motion changes to the curriculum to rectify this. All of this amounted to a concerted effort to 'put a kilt' on the Scottish Tories: an attempt to change the image of the party north of the border by becoming more Scottish and divorcing 'Scottishness' from support for constitutional change.

The Conservatives remained hostile to devolution. In 1992, John Major spoke with more conviction on this than any other matter:

> If I could summon up all the authority of this office, I would put it into this single warning – the United Kingdom is in danger. Wake up, my fellow countrymen! Wake up now before it is too late![30]

By the late 1980s, the Conservatives' grip on politics north of the border had become wholly dependent on the success of the party in England. There are a number of reasons for Tory-unionist opposition to devolution, yet simple expediency is important. The party is currently in a minority and looks unlikely, in the foreseeable future, to build up its support to the levels it achieved forty years ago. Its electoral base and level of support would have to expand fairly dramatically before it would have much hope of power in a Scottish Parliament. Not only is there little prospect of it winning an overall majority in a Scottish Parliament, but no other party could afford to be in coalition with it for fear of losing support amongst its supporters. The Conservatives have allowed themselves to become the pariahs of mainstream Scottish politics.

In terms of their understanding of the United Kingdom, support for devolution would also present problems for the Conservatives. Under Michael Forsyth, Conservative rhetoric and actions suggested a more pluralist understanding of Britain: a move back to an understanding of Scotland as part of a union, rather than a unitary state. But Forsyth's initiatives were limited, rhetorical and superficial.

Symbolic gestures rather than substantive concessions were offered. The underlying impression remained that of a party which viewed Britain as a unitary state. It may not have been the assimilationist unitary model of Margaret Thatcher but neither was it the dynamic union state model.

The Scottish Tory 'wipe-out' in 1997 was as unexpected as the slight revival in the party's fortunes had been in 1992. There were two explanations for the dramatic outcome of the election: there were the effects of long-term decline, largely due to the failure of the party in Scotland to articulate a Scottish message, and there was also the more immediate impact of divisions in the party across Britain and the general anti-Government mood of the British electorate. The latter would probably be overcome in time in opposition; the former would require some attention. New problems emerged compounding difficulties in articulating a Scottish message. The Tories had no Scottish figure and no Scottish issue around which to rally. Devolution looked certain. To oppose it would make it more difficult to recover. To embrace devolution would be unconvincing, having spent eighteen years arguing that it would lead to the break up of Britain. The 1997 election not only deprived the Tories of any Scottish MPs but the election of a Labour Government presented the party with a wholly new set of problems.

The challenge for the Scottish Conservatives is to find a convincing articulation of union-state unionism. As part of this challenge they will have to take account of the changing context. Changes in society and government have territorial implications. New contexts demand new responses. The union state requires to have new life breathed into it, and it may take more than a few symbolic gestures to satisfy Scottish demands. Conservatives have argued against a Scottish Parliament on the grounds that it would fundamentally alter the territorial balance within Britain. When it is established they will be forced to confront a difficult situation. The Scottish Tories will require a major re-invention of themselves, far greater than anything seen so far.

Labour and Unionism

Just as the Conservatives have traditionally associated with a union state interpretation of the UK, so too has Labour, in a more limited way, over the post-war period. The 'peasant's stockpot' of ideas in the earlier years of Labour's history had included Scottish nationalism, but this was later overshadowed by late Fabian paternalist central-ism.[31] Centralists and paternalists such as Sidney and Beatrice Webb dominated the battle of ideas in the early- to mid-twentieth century, with the more decentralist, participatory and developmental ethos of Guild Socialists such as G. D. H. Cole playing a secondary role. In policy terms, post-war Labour was committed to centralised demand management and nationalised industries. The extension of state activities did not take account of Scottish distinctiveness as previ-ously, indeed, pensions and social security were delivered uniformly.

This was not a policy of conscious assimilation so much as a series of social and economic policies which had assimilationist conse-quences. The development of the welfare state, nationalisation and planning all gave a greater role to the state. However, the policies associated with this increased state activity were largely controlled from the centre. The Scottish Office did not lose powers and respon-sibilities so much as it failed to gain new ones. The Scottish compo-nent was diminished, but the state at the centre acquired more power. The challenge for the Labour Party was to find means of increasing the powers of the state while maintaining the balance within the union state.

Home rule agitation in the immediate post-war period focused on the increasing role of the state and its implications for Scotland in the union. Attlee's cabinet discussed the agitation and acknowledged the sincerity of those demanding home rule and the dilemmas faced. Indeed, Labour had fought the 1945 election with a commitment to set up a Scottish Parliament. However, in opposition, the Scottish Unionists played up the centralist implications of nationalisation. Just as Labour did in opposition, the Tories played the 'Scottish card' to the embarrassment of the Government. In a memorandum to cabinet colleagues after the 1950 general election, Hector McNeil, Secretary of State for Scotland, noted that the feeling that national-isation equalled centralisation was strong in Scotland and that Labour was 'particularly vulnerable' in the case of electricity.[32]

The Attlee Government issued a white paper in 1948.[33] In impor-tant respects it resembled similar documents within the union state tradition of unionism produced over the years by the Conservatives. It acknowledged the 'widespread desire in Scotland that the Scottish people should have increased opportunities of dealing with affairs of purely Scottish concern.'[34] The problem was finding new means of doing this. Proposals to reform parliamentary business, management of the economy, the machinery of government and nationalised industries and the possibility of some kind of enquiry were discussed. Changes in Parliamentary procedures were instituted. Another of the proposals which was put into effect was the establishment of a Scottish Economic Conference, meeting under the chairmanship of the Secretary of State for Scotland, with representatives from industry, commerce, trade unions, nationalised industries and government departments. The conference was, as was much else, more symbolic than substantive. Almost fifty years later, Michael Forsyth revived the Scottish Economic Conference in his attempt to meet the demands for greater control of Scottish affairs. Once more, symbolic politics was an important part of the response coming from the Government.

Labour's commitment to a Scottish Parliament only existed in theory between 1945 and 1957. In January 1957, the executive committee of the Scottish Council of the Labour Party came out against home rule on 'compelling economic grounds'. Labour could not reconcile home rule with central demand management of the economy. Centralist thinking dominated Labour politics around this time. This did not mean that the party supported the assimilation of Scotland into England. Rather, it meant that the Scottish dimension had to be catered for through symbolic gestures and extending existing arrangements.

As Harold Wilson's Scottish Secretary from 1964 to 1970 and again from 1974 until Wilson's resignation as Prime Minister in 1976, Willie Ross was the most significant post-war Labour politician in Scotland. Ross held the view that the Scottish Office was the best means through which Scottish interests could be expressed. He was by no means an assimilationist and vigorously opposed any effort made by fellow cabinet members to intrude into Scottish business. His jealous guard of his own domain was noted by Richard Crossman in his diaries.[35] It was a paternalist version of union-state unionism with a strong unitary state strand, the latter being evident in Labour's support for centralised demand management and a centralised model of the welfare state.

A *volte face* on devolution was forced on Labour when the SNP threatened its electoral base in the 1970s. Significantly, the decision to support a devolved Scottish assembly was taken in London and was effectively imposed on the Labour Party in Scotland. In August 1974, Labour in Scotland reluctantly agreed to support legislative devolution at a special conference. There had always been a pro-home rule element in the party in Scotland but these people had been marginalised. John Mackintosh, academic and maverick MP, gave strong backing to Scottish devolution, but the party was divided on the issue and a number of prominent figures opposed the new policy. Scottish Labour did not embrace the policy but accepted it reluctantly as a means of undermining the SNP.

A major concession made to anti-devolutionists within the Parliamentary Labour Party was the inclusion of a referendum clause in the devolution legislation passed by Parliament. The clause was amended, with crucial support coming from the Labour benches, to add a '40 per cent rule'. This required the Secretary of State to move a repeal order on the legislation in the event of less than 40 per cent of the eligible electorate voting for devolution. This proved too high a hurdle for campaigners. The Government were obliged to move the repeal order, though not obliged to vote for it. In the event, James Callaghan's Labour Government did not dare move the repeal order for fear that it would expose the divisions within the parliamentary party and the extent of opposition to devolution so near to an election. The chief whip informed Callaghan that he could not rely on his own backbenchers.[36] The SNP and Liberals voted with the Tories in a vote of confidence precipitating a general election which saw the return of the Conservatives under Margaret Thatcher. The Tories repealed the devolution legislation and for a period, that seemed the end of it.

However, the election of the Tories under Margaret Thatcher only temporarily killed off devolution as an issue. Indeed, it caused some important changes in Labour Party thinking on the constitution. Scottish Labour came to embrace a Scottish Parliament. This has involved a change in their interpretation of the nature of Britain and Labour unionism. The most significant change came in 1989 when all Scottish Labour MPs, apart from Tam Dalyell, signed the 'Claim of Right for Scotland' – a document drawn up by a cross-party home rule body. The document asserted the 'sovereign right of the Scottish people to determine the form of Government best suited to their needs'.[37] For a period Scottish Labour argued for 'independence in the UK', though Gerald Kaufman, a senior front-bench Labour politician, had obviously not been told of this when on a visit to Scotland in 1989 he dismissed the notion.[38]

There are a number of reasons why Labour's position changed. Labour members saw whole areas of Scottish life transformed while their party was impotent to prevent this, despite having the overwhelming support of the Scottish people. Labour housing authorities, for example, saw their stocks dwindle and deteriorate. It was thought that many services which would have been the responsibility of a Scottish Assembly might have been protected.

Often associated with local government, where Labour retained a power base, a more radical decentralist strand of thinking reemerged in the early 1980s. The Conservative Government's decision to abolish the Greater London Council and English Metropolitan Councils suggested to many people in the Labour Party that there had to be something in having an intermediate tier of government if Margaret Thatcher was so intent on getting rid of it.[39] Municipal socialism came into its own in the era, with novel ways of resisting Conservative policies and advancing programmes for job-creation and the protection of services. Local socialism in the 1980s has been described as the reaction to four crises: the fiscal crisis in local government; the social crisis of the inner cities; the electoral crisis of the Labour Party and the ideological crisis of socialism.[40] When the national dimension is added to this list, it is little wonder that the conditions of the early 1980s should result in Scottish Labour embracing devolution. The centralist, unitary state thinking which had tended to dominate was challenged.

However, the early 1980s also saw the emergence of Labour's Alternative Economic Strategy (AES) which involved fairly large scale, centralist policy-making. This seemed to require a view of Britain as a unitary state. Although an Alternative Regional Strategy was drawn up by John Prescott, it never succeeded in reconciling Labour's centralist demand-management outlook (which required a unitary state perspective), with the more decentralist union-state perspective of the growing home rule lobby within the party in Scotland. The 1983 election result ended the leftward drift of the Labour Party and the AES. Over time, under Neil Kinnock and more particularly under Tony Blair, Labour abandoned any residual support for nationalisation, central-demand management and many of the key policies which had influenced Labour's centralist unitary state perspective. It was ironic that a move was started under Kinnock, a vehement opponent of devolution in the 1970s, which removed many of the impediments in the way of Labour's commitment to devolution.

The changes brought about through the 'modernisation' of the Labour Party and the creation of 'New Labour' had contradictory consequences. A far more centralised party organisation emerged with power increasingly concentrated in the leadership. Constitutionally, power in the Labour Party had long been held at the centre, but the Scottish Council of the Labour Party (renamed the Scottish Labour Party in 1994) had some informal autonomy. An easy relationship existed between Labour's formal constitutional structure and its informal arrangements. To a large extent, Scottish Labour's more radical conference resolutions were indulgently put up with by the party leadership, and so long as the party was winning elections,' it was allowed a fair degree of informal autonomy. Under Blair, however, the formal structures and informal arrangements came into conflict with the former winning out. The party's autonomy north of the border was increasingly circumscribed. The Labour Party appeared more centralised – analogous with conforming to a unitary state model – than at any stage in its history.

On the other hand, many of the public policies which required tight central control were comprehensively abandoned. The old problem of reconciling Labour policies with the union state were lessened while power was centralised inside the party. Labour's drift to the right has made devolution far more compatible with its economic policy, though less compatible with the new style of party management.

The negative reasons for Labour's support for devolution did not disappear. The continued electoral threat posed by the SNP concentrated Labour minds. Superficially, the SNP appeared less of a threat in the 1980s than in the 1970s. It did less well in elections, but in the 1980s it was building a coherent base of support. By the 1992 election, the SNP support resembled Labour's. It had largely become a working-class party with broadly left-wing supporters. Like its voters, the SNP itself had a more explicitly left-wing image especially when compared to its support and image in the 1970s. Significantly, it was the second choice of a substantial number of Labour voters and closer to Labour than any other party. It posed a greater threat than at any time in the past.[41]

Labour's most vehement critics of devolution in the past based their opposition on an assumption that the UK was a unitary state. Tam Dalyell's many contributions to debates in the 1970s exemplify this thinking. During the second reading of the Scotland Bill in November 1977 he criticised the Conservatives' support for devolution, claiming that it would be more honest to admit that it was impossible to have an Assembly – especially any kind of subordinate Parliament – that is part, though only part, of a unitary state.'[42]

Dalyell was correct in identifying the incompatibility of devolution in a unitary state but he was wrong in describing the UK as a unitary state.

Labour, however, remains confused on this point, as reflected in its responses to the so-called 'West Lothian Question'. In January 1995, Gordon Brown adopted a unitary state perspective when he argued that a Scottish Parliament and Welsh Assembly 'go hand in hand with the offer of greater regional democracy throughout Britain' and that this meant that the West Lothian Question was not a barrier to change.[43] In other words, symmetry was seen as important. Tony Blair based his response on a union state conception of the UK (even if he did not know it at the time), when he argued two months later that he did not see Scottish devolution 'in any shape of form dependent upon what happens in the English regions'.[44] However, his unilateral decision to have a two question referendum in Summer 1996 suggested that he had adopted a unitary state view of Britain. By far the most confused was Jack Straw, who had overall responsibility for regional government, and who managed to combine both unitary and union state in his utterances simultaneously. This has resulted in a great deal of confusion within the Labour Party on the issue.

Scottish Labour has moved dramatically since the 1970s. The decision to change the official name of the party the Scottish Labour Party and the continuing pressure for greater party autonomy (though strongly resisted) are evidence of change. The question, however, is whether Scottish Labour has really converted English Labour. Labour needed to win England to win the 1997 election and did so with a landslide. The success in building a broad coalition of support in opposition paid huge electoral dividends. The challenge for the Blair Government would be to retain the support of that coalition. One aspect of this is the territorial dimension. Blair cannot afford to be seen to favour Scotland but must deliver a measure of Scottish home rule and respond to the various pressures from Wales and some English regions. A new conception of Britain is likely to emerge throughout the state. Whether this satisfies the Scots or merely whets their appetite depends on whether Britain is perceived to be working again. Many Scots came to believe that Britain under the Conservatives did not work for them. The challenge for Blair is to convince Scots that this was a failure of the Conservatives not a failure of Britain.

Conclusion

One of the key changes in Scottish politics over the last thirty years has been within the unionist camp. It seems that unionism is less coherent than it once was. It is no longer possible to talk of unionism as if it is one cohesive force. Many of those who belong to what might be described as the union-state school have more in common with Scottish nationalists. This reflects changes both in the nature of these ideologies and also the international context in which they exist. It was argued at the outset that unionism is a form of nationalism and that nationalism is contingent. Absolutist notions of sovereignty were never convincing but look increasingly absurd.[45]

The balance of opinion within the Labour and Conservative parties has altered over time. In part, this is a function of opposition: the longer a party remains in opposition, the more it plays the 'Scottish card'. Labour rediscovered its Scottish (nationalist) roots in the 1980s and moved from reluctant acceptance of a policy of devolution to embrace a policy of Scottish self-determination. The Scottish dimension was stressed increasingly during the Thatcher years but debate on Scotland's constitutional status within the Labour Party was very parochial. Few in the party in England knew or cared about Scottish devolution until Blair became leader. The danger of Labour being portrayed as a party of the Celtic peripheries; the need to appeal to 'middle England'; and attacks on the tax-varying powers of the proposed Parliament, resulted in London taking an interest in the policy. The depth of Labour's commitment has been seriously tested during Tony Blair's leadership. Blair's knowledge of the debate on Scotland's constitutional status on becoming leader was meagre and his sympathy for Scottish aspirations has at times proved shallow. Without the baggage of hostility to devolution which hindered Neil Kinnock and with a driving ambition to reach Downing Street, Blair was able to move his party back towards traditional unionism, though even he has not dared to throw the party's commitment to devolution over-board entirely. The change was exemplified in the rhetoric adopted by George Robertson as Shadow Scottish Secretary. Whereas Donald Dewar talked about 'independence in the UK', Robertson referred to a 'New Unionism'. The real test of any party's understanding of the territorial politics of Britain comes only when it is in power. The appointment of Donald Dewar as Secretary of State for Scotland after the 1997 election suggested a more positive attitude to change. Nonetheless, as Labour moved closer to power, the unitary state conception of Britain had been reasserted. The divisions within unionism within the Labour party look no more settled today than in the past.

The Conservatives were the unionists *par excellence* though the nature of unionism within the party has changed over time. Under Margaret Thatcher an understanding of Britain which informed policy emerged which was almost assimilationist. This harmed the Scottish Tories. Attempts since Mrs Thatcher's demise to revive traditional unionism have been unsuccessful in terms of winning the hearts and minds of the Scottish electorate.

In contemporary debates, unionism and nationalism are presented as if they are mutually exclusive ideologies; one asserting the 'sovereignty of Parliament' against another asserting the 'sovereignty of the Scottish people'. In fact, there are many variants of unionism and in one form it closely resembles Scottish nationalism. Indeed, unionism in any of its forms is a form of nationalism – a collective identity. The real issue is its composition. That remains contested.

NOTES

1. Benedict Anderson, *Imaged Communities: Reflections of the Origin and Spread of Nationalism* (London, 1991), pp. 6, 7.
2. Michael Keating, *State and Regional Nationalism* (Hemel Hempstead, 1988).
3. James G. Kellas, *The Politics of Nationalism and Ethnicity* (Houndmills, 1991), pp. 51–52
4. It could, of course, be argued that there are no UK citizens but rather that there are UK subjects.
5. Richard Rose, *Understanding the United Kingdom* (London, 1982), p. 11.
6. Michael Billig, *Banal Nationalism* (London, 1995), p. 6. Billig's definition is similar to the classic definition offered by Ernest Renan in 1882 who suggested in *Qu'est-ce qu-une nation?* that nations had a sense of common past and a present will to live together. The existence of a nation is a 'daily plebiscite'. E. Renan, 'What is a nation?' in Alfred Zimmern (ed.), *Modern Political Doctrines* (Oxford, 1939), p. 203.
7. John Breuilly, 'Sovereignty and boundaries: modern state formation and national identity in Germany', in Mary Fulbrook (ed.), *National Histories and European History* (London, 1993), pp. 94–140. John Breuilly, *Nationalism and the State*, Second Edition, (Manchester, 1993), Ch. 4.
8. Michael Keating, *State and Regional Nationalism* (London, 1988), p. 1.
9. Eugen Weber, *Peasants into Frenchmen: The Modernisation of Rural France* (London, 1977).
10. *Ibid.*, p. 486.
11. Linda Colley, *Britons: Forging the Nation, 1707–1837* (London, 1992).

12. Robert Michels, 'Conservatism', *Encyclopaedia of the Social Sciences*, Vol.4, (1930).
13. Lindsay Paterson, *The Autonomy of Scotland* (Edinburgh, 1994).
14. For the threat posed by the SNP to Labour's electoral base see Lynn Bennie, Jack Brand and James Mitchell, *How Scotland Votes* (Manchester, 1997).
15. James Mitchell, *Conservatives and the Union* (Edinburgh, 1990) Ch. 5.
16. Neil MacCormick, *Legal Reasoning and Legal Theory* (Oxford, 1978), pp. 130. See also T.B. Smith, 'The Union of 1707 as fundamental law', *Public Law*, Summer (1957), pp. 99–121.
17. I have used the union state and unitary state distinction in a number of contexts. See, for example, James Mitchell, *Strategies for Self-Government* (Edinburgh, 1996), pp. 37–43. Others have followed since. Gerry Hassan, 'New Labour and the Politics of Scotland' in Mark Perryman (ed.), *The Blair Agenda* (London, 1996), pp. 170–197; Constitution Unit, *Scotland's Parliament: Fundamentals for a New Scotland Act* (London, 1996).
18. Derek Urwin, 'The Development of the Conservative Organisation in Scotland Until 1912', *Scottish Historical Review* 44 (1965), pp. 89–111.; 'Scottish Conservatism: A Party Organisation in Transition', *Political Studies* 14 (1966), pp. 145–162.
19. '"Psychic income" refers to those things which satisfy the mental and spiritual needs of human beings; material interests are those things which are readily quantifiable in cash terms, such as incomes and jobs.' James Kellas, *The Politics of Nationalism and Ethnicity* (Houndmills, 1991), pp. 66–67.
20. See, for example, R. J. Finlay, 'Unionism and the Dependency Culture: Politics and State Intervention in Scotland, 1918–1987' in this volume.
21. Michael Oakeshott, *Rationalism in Politics* (London, 1962); Anthony Quinton, *The Politics of Imperfection* (London, 1978); Quinton Hogg, *The Case for Conservatism* (London, 1978).
22. HMSO, *Report of the Committee on Scottish Administration*, Cmnd. 5563, (1937).
23. Ian Lang and Barry Henderson, *The Scottish Conservatives: A Past and a Future* (Edinburgh (Scottish Conservative and Unionist Association), 1975). Another example was the *Royal Commission on Scottish Affairs*, which reported in 1954. (HMSO, Cmnd. 9212, (1954)).
24. Conservative submission published in *Report of the Hansard Commission on Election Campaigns* (London, 1991).
25. James Mitchell and Lynn Bennie, 'Thatcherism and the Scottish Question', in C. Rawlings, D. M. Farrell, D. Denver and D. Broughton (eds), *British Elections and Parties Yearbook 1995* (London, 1996), pp. 90–104.
26. Jim Bulpitt, 'The Discipline of the New Democracy: Mrs Thatcher's Domestic Statecraft', *Political Studies* (1986), p. 21.
27. Bennie, Brand and Mitchell, *How Scotland Votes*, pp. 131–142.
28. HMSO, *Scotland in the Union – a partnership for good*, Cmnd. 2225 (March 1993).
29. The Stone is part of nationalist folklore. According to legend, it had been used as the coronation stone of Scottish monarchs until Edward I took it

to London in the middle ages. In modern times, it was part of the coronation stone of modern monarchs. A group of students removed it from Westminster Abbey in 1950 and returned it to Scotland. This student prank caused great amusement in Scotland and considerable consternation in London. See Mitchell, *Strategies for Self-Government*, pp. 159–266.

30. Quoted in David Butler and Dennis Kavanagh, *The British General Election of 1992* (Houndmills, 1992), p. 130.
31. Frank Bealey, *The Social and Political Thought of the British Labour Party* (London, 1970), Introduction.
32. Public Records Office, Cabinet papers, CP(50) 101, *Scottish Affairs* memorandum by Hector McNeil, 11 May 1950.
33. Scottish Home Department, *Scottish Affairs*, Cmnd. 7308, (1948)
34. *Ibid.*, p. 2, para.1.
35. Richard Crossman, *Diaries of a Cabinet Minister*, Vol.2, (London, 1977), pp. 550–551.
36. James Callaghan, *Time and Chance* (London, 1988), p.560.
37. Scottish Constitutional Convention, *Claim of Right for Scotland*, signed at the inaugural meeting of the Scottish Constitutional Convention, 30 March 1989.
38. Iain Macwhirter, 'After Doomsday...The Convention and Scotland's Constitutional Crisis', *Scottish Government Yearbook 1990* (Edinburgh, 1990), pp. 21–34.
39. Norman Flynn, Steve Leach, Carol Vielba, *Abolition or Reform? The GLC and the Metropolitan Councils* (London, 1985).
40. John Gyford, *The Politics of Local Socialism* (London, 1985), p. 95.
41. Jack Brand, James Mitchell, Paula Surridge, 'Social Constituency and Ideological Profile: Scottish Nationalism in the 1990s', *Political Studies*, 42 (1994), pp. 616–629; 'Will Scotland Come to the Aid of the Party?' in A. Heath et. al. (eds), *Labour's Last Chance? The 1992 Election and Beyond* (Aldershot, 1994), pp. 213–228.
42. Hansard, Commons, Tam Dalyell, 14 Nov. 1977, Vol. 939, cols. 78–79.
43. Speech delivered by Gordon Brown MP, 12 Jan. 1995.
44. *The Scotsman*, 8 March 1995.
45. James Mitchell, 'Shibboleths and Slogans: Sovereignty, Subsidiarity and Constitutional Debate', *Scottish Government Yearbook 1992* (Edinburgh, 1992), pp.98–113.

INDEX

140